Making Sense of Modern Science

Einstein's theory of relativity, the butterfly effect, deep learning, game theory. If you've heard these buzzwords but are a bit fuzzy on the details, then this book is for you. Professor Lev Reyzin will take you on a fascinating whirlwind tour of the science behind these concepts, answering your burning questions about Pangea, DNA, and what exactly quantum computing is. Using clear language and emphasizing big ideas over technical details, this book shows that science can be enjoyed by everyone. Each chapter explores a different foundational scientific idea, ending with a brief history of the topic, further reading, and more technical details for the mathematically inclined reader. Much of science is developed through curiosity about the world around us, and this book will help feed that curiosity in you.

Lev Reyzin is a professor at the University of Illinois Chicago whose research spans mathematics, theoretical computer science, and artificial intelligence. He co-directs the National Science Foundation-funded IDEAL Institute and is Editor-in-Chief of the *Mathematics of Data, Learning, and Intelligence* journal. His work has received multiple awards at leading machine learning venues.

"Lev Reyzin takes readers on a whirlwind tour of a few fascinating topics in modern science. Anyone interested in science not professionally, but as a crucial branch of human culture, will find something engaging and thought-provoking in this book."

MARIO LIVIO, astrophysicist, author of *The Golden Ratio* and *Is God A Mathematician?*

"You would not expect to sit down to a bite-sized book of 185 pages and come away with a coherent understanding of game theory, plate tectonics, quantum mechanics, and neural nets. Prepare to be agreeably surprised by Lev Reyzin's *Making Sense of Modern Science*, a remarkable feat of clear, concise scientific erudition."

JORDAN ELLENBERG, University of Wisconsin, author of *How Not to Be Wrong* and *Shape*

Making Sense of Modern Science

A Tour for the Curious

Lev Reyzin

University of Illinois Chicago

CAMBRIDGE
UNIVERSITY PRESS

CAMBRIDGE
UNIVERSITY PRESS

Shaftesbury Road, Cambridge CB2 8EA, United Kingdom
One Liberty Plaza, 20th Floor, New York, NY 10006, USA
477 Williamstown Road, Port Melbourne, VIC 3207, Australia
314–321, 3rd Floor, Plot 3, Splendor Forum, Jasola District Centre,
New Delhi – 110025, India

Cambridge University Press is part of Cambridge University Press & Assessment,
a department of the University of Cambridge.

We share the University's mission to contribute to society through the pursuit of
education, learning and research at the highest international levels of excellence.

www.cambridge.org
Information on this title: www.cambridge.org/9781009711197
DOI: 10.1017/9781009711210

When citing this work, please include a reference to the DOI 10.1017/9781009711210

First published 2027

Cover image: Olga Kalantarov Hautin

A catalogue record for this publication is available from the British Library

A Cataloging-in-Publication data record for this book is available from the Library of Congress

ISBN 978-1-009-71119-7 Paperback

To Sammy and Abby,
who I hope will enjoy this book in the due course of time.

Contents

Preface

The idea for this book came about after a conversation I had with a friend about what her son, then in high school, might want to study in college. He was generally interested in math and science, so we discussed possible colleges for him to consider and majors he might eventually pursue. She told me that she was encouraged by my excitement about the intellectual adventures that awaited him. To help spark his interest in specific subjects, I decided to find a good book to recommend – something that offered a lucid account of modern scientific insights. To my surprise, I could not find the kind of book I had expected to exist.

I realized that in imagining such a book, I already had concrete ideas about at least some of the topics it should cover. Over the years, I had accumulated ways of looking at different scientific ideas that exposed their core insights while also conveying the bigger picture. I had refined these explanations over time through many conversations – after which people often told me they wished they had encountered these descriptions earlier.

After some more searching, I finally concluded that if a book were to exist that addressed the topics I thought needed to be covered, I would have to write it. The prospect of taking on this project filled me with excitement, and true to my academic instincts, I was eager to add my own perspective on certain topics. As a computer scientist by training, this perspective sometimes involved seeing the natural sciences through a computational lens.

The hardest part of writing this book was deciding which topics to include and which to skip. I tried to follow four main principles:

the topics needed to be important; an elegant insight had to lie at their center; the ideas needed to be accepted by the scientific community; and the science had to be intelligible to nonexperts. Each of these considerations necessitated the difficult decision to exclude some otherwise fascinating subjects. I have no doubt that some readers would have made some different decisions, but I hope they will not hold that against me.

The book that finally emerged contains what I believe to be some of the most profound scientific insights of approximately the last hundred years. It is meant not just for high school students curious about what science has to offer but also for adults who want to learn about modern scientific ideas. Even specialists in a given area may find something new in chapters covering topics outside their own fields – I certainly ran into many delightful surprises while working on this book.

A final note: Each chapter ends with an optional "Further Explorations" section. Readers interested in the history of science will probably enjoy the "Historical Notes," while the "For the Mathematically Inclined" is aimed primarily at those for whom this resonates. Most will probably want to skip the mathematics, perhaps to return to it at a later point. Anyone especially drawn to a topic is encouraged to explore the books listed under "Additional Reading."

I hope you enjoy reading this book as much as I enjoyed writing it. Welcome to what I hope will be an exciting scientific journey!

Preface

The idea for this book came about after a conversation I had with a friend about what her son, then in high school, might want to study in college. He was generally interested in math and science, so we discussed possible colleges for him to consider and majors he might eventually pursue. She told me that she was encouraged by my excitement about the intellectual adventures that awaited him. To help spark his interest in specific subjects, I decided to find a good book to recommend – something that offered a lucid account of modern scientific insights. To my surprise, I could not find the kind of book I had expected to exist.

I realized that in imagining such a book, I already had concrete ideas about at least some of the topics it should cover. Over the years, I had accumulated ways of looking at different scientific ideas that exposed their core insights while also conveying the bigger picture. I had refined these explanations over time through many conversations – after which people often told me they wished they had encountered these descriptions earlier.

After some more searching, I finally concluded that if a book were to exist that addressed the topics I thought needed to be covered, I would have to write it. The prospect of taking on this project filled me with excitement, and true to my academic instincts, I was eager to add my own perspective on certain topics. As a computer scientist by training, this perspective sometimes involved seeing the natural sciences through a computational lens.

The hardest part of writing this book was deciding which topics to include and which to skip. I tried to follow four main principles:

the topics needed to be important; an elegant insight had to lie at their center; the ideas needed to be accepted by the scientific community; and the science had to be intelligible to nonexperts. Each of these considerations necessitated the difficult decision to exclude some otherwise fascinating subjects. I have no doubt that some readers would have made some different decisions, but I hope they will not hold that against me.

The book that finally emerged contains what I believe to be some of the most profound scientific insights of approximately the last hundred years. It is meant not just for high school students curious about what science has to offer but also for adults who want to learn about modern scientific ideas. Even specialists in a given area may find something new in chapters covering topics outside their own fields – I certainly ran into many delightful surprises while working on this book.

A final note: Each chapter ends with an optional "Further Explorations" section. Readers interested in the history of science will probably enjoy the "Historical Notes," while the "For the Mathematically Inclined" is aimed primarily at those for whom this resonates. Most will probably want to skip the mathematics, perhaps to return to it at a later point. Anyone especially drawn to a topic is encouraged to explore the books listed under "Additional Reading."

I hope you enjoy reading this book as much as I enjoyed writing it. Welcome to what I hope will be an exciting scientific journey!

1

Introduction
Modern Ideas in Science

Since the dawn of mankind, humanity has discovered an astounding amount about itself and the world. In just 10,000 years, *Homo sapiens* have gone from living in caves to transforming the planet. Humanity's journey from using primitive tools to launching spacecraft into orbit and beyond is a testament to human ingenuity and capacity for creating powerful explanatory frameworks.

This process of development is not simply a gradual accumulation of data. Science has progressed through the emergence of new insights, often revolutionary in their time, though eventually absorbed into the body of common knowledge. Here are just a few examples:

- *The shape of the world*: The notion that the world is round was first conjectured by Aristotle in the fourth century BCE based on the circular shape of lunar eclipses. Soon after, Eratosthenes accurately calculated the circumference of the Earth using the angles of shadows. This insight was radical because it required accepting an abstract model of the world that contradicted everyday perception. Today, this truth is easily confirmed by boarding a plane.

- *The planets orbit the Sun*: In the sixteenth century, Copernicus developed the simpler heliocentric model to explain planetary orbits, and his model was later bolstered by Galileo and Kepler. His insight challenged both intuition and religious dogma and fundamentally changed humanity's understanding of its place in the universe. While this is harder to confirm personally, the Earth's tilted axis, together with its revolution around the Sun, forms a simple and compelling explanation for the seasons, rooted in Earth's orbit and tilt.
- *Evolution by natural selection*: In the mid-nineteenth century, Darwin and Wallace gave a compelling theory of biological evolution that offered a powerful mechanism to explain the diversity of life, without appealing to divine purpose or design. Natural selection gives a beautiful and parsimonious explanation of many phenomena surrounding the variety of life on Earth.

Though even these basic insights still have their doubters (flat-Earthers, contemporary geocentrists, and creationists, respectively), they are broadly accepted and representative of ideas that have long entered common knowledge. Other widely understood theories include Newton's laws of motion, the germ theory of disease, and the periodic table's explanation of element properties. Some more complex concepts – such as thermodynamics and electromagnetism – have widespread awareness, even if most people are hazy on their details.

All of these theories, however, are well over a century old. When it comes to the great ideas of the twentieth century, people are less informed. They may have heard of the "Big Bang," $E = mc^2$, and the "butterfly effect," but this knowledge is usually superficial. Other topics, like quantum mechanics or computational complexity, are often seen as too hard to explain. Even worse, in popular accounts they are often bungled, leaving readers confused or misinformed.

The mathematics involved in quantum mechanics, relativistic electrodynamics, or computational complexity is indeed more difficult than the equations governing Newton's laws of motion,* but the underlying ideas of these fields are not only possible to grasp but also form a bigger picture that is elegant and accessible. These modern theories, despite their mathematical complexity, ultimately reveal a deeper, more unified understanding of the physical world.

The twentieth century witnessed an explosion of new ideas wholly unlike those seen in the science of previous centuries. Einstein's theory of relativity reexamined the nature of time, quantum mechanics overturned classical notions of physical reality, and Gödel's theory of incompleteness exposed inherent limits on mathematical reasoning. These developments revealed that uncertainty and incompleteness are not merely epistemic limitations but fundamental aspects of nature itself. A striking unifying pattern across these fields showed that seemingly simple rules and principles can generate extraordinary complexity, while computation emerged as a fundamental and ubiquitous process underlying physical reality, biological systems, and human thought. This computational perspective has culminated in recent advances in artificial intelligence and machine learning, prompting society to reconsider broader questions surrounding what it means to be human.

These modern scientific insights have yielded profound practical applications that shape contemporary life. Quantum mechanics underpins technologies from lasers to magnetic resonance imaging (MRI), relativity provides time corrections essential for the global positioning system (GPS), molecular genetics advances medicine

* It is worth noting that to apply these laws, Newton had to develop calculus, but even calculus is taught in secondary school.

through gene therapies and personalized treatments, and information theory drives the internet protocols used by billions daily. In addition to their abstract beauty, these ideas provide an invisible scaffolding to twenty-first-century life, enabling capabilities that previous generations would have considered miraculous.

This book aims to demystify the ideas behind these and other modern intellectual triumphs. Each chapter focuses on a different idea or set of related ideas.* All of these are scientific ideas in the comprehensive sense of the term. A broad view of science appreciates that reasoning and explanation play as much of a role in scientific understanding and progress as the discovery of physical laws. In this encompassing sense, areas of computation, game theory, and mathematics present key scientific insights, some of which are represented within these chapters. Appreciating the topics herein requires some thoughtful reflection and an open mind, but the intellectual rewards are well worth the effort.

* Though some of the chapters involve connected ideas, they are presented in a way that they can be read independently. It is, however, recommended to read them in order.

2

On the Edge of Certainty

Chaos Theory

In 1972, the meteorologist and chaos theory pioneer Edward Lorenz gave a talk to the American Association for the Advancement of Science under the title "Does the Flap of a Butterfly's Wings in Brazil Set Off a Tornado in Texas?"[1] By now, it is commonly accepted that such an eventuality is indeed possible, and the striking image of a mere butterfly causing a violent storm gave rise to the now-famous term the *butterfly effect*.

It is not hard to imagine a small occurrence having large repercussions in human events. For example, a butterfly can tickle someone's ear, and he might turn to wave the butterfly away, only to avoid a bullet. If that person is important enough, that event can change the course of history, let alone cause a tornado. It seems more surprising that similarly large consequences can occur in purely *physical systems*, real-world systems governed by the equations of nature rather than by human or animal behavior. But in fact, systems where small changes cannot cause large effects are more the exception than the rule. This chapter aims to explain this surprising phenomenon and what it signifies.

Deterministic Unpredictability

As Chapter 5 will explain, measurements of certain properties of quantum systems can yield probabilistic outcomes. The spin of an electron is one such property, and it is therefore unsurprising that the result of its measurement can be unpredictable, as is anything that relies on its outcome. One can even buy a quantum random number generator for applications like cryptography or gambling, where provable sources of randomness are desired.

Quantum randomness is truly unpredictable – not just in practice but according to the very laws of nature. Chaos theory, however, reveals something quite different: Determinism, where the future is in principle fixed, does not guarantee predictability in practice. The following formula, called a *logistic map*, illustrates the phenomenon of a very simple equation behaving unpredictably:

$$x_{n+1} = rx_n(1 - x_n),$$

where r can be set to an arbitrary value. For the present analysis, $r = 4$ can be used, obtaining the equation $x_{n+1} = 4x_n(1 - x_n)$. This equation takes a starting value at x_0 and can then be used to produce subsequent values. For example if $x_0 = 0.3$, then $x_1 = 4 \times 0.3 \times 0.7 = 0.84$. Now x_1 can be used to find $x_2 = 4 \times 0.84 \times 0.16 = 0.5376$, and so on. This creates a sequence of numbers $x_0, x_1, x_2, \ldots$

One can now compute two different series with almost identical start values for x_0. The first series will start with the value 0.4 and the second with the almost identical value 0.400001, and

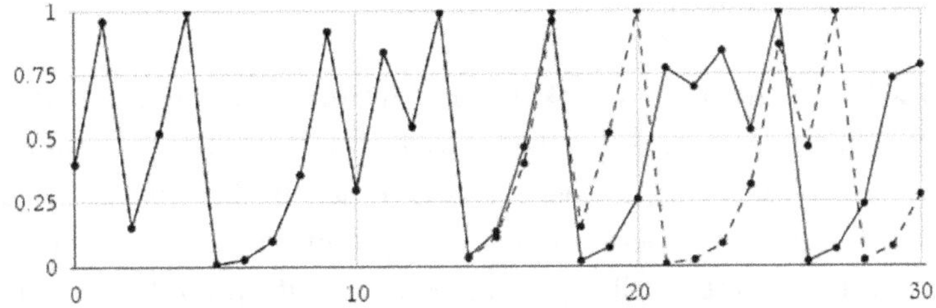

Figure 2.1 Iterations of the logistic map $x_{n+1} = 4x_n(1 - x_n)$ for two initial conditions, $x_0 = 0.4$ (solid line) and $x_0 = 0.400001$ (dashed line). Values of n are on the x-axis, and values of x are on the y-axis.

their difference is tiny, only 10^{-6}. Figure 2.1 illustrates that while the difference between the two series is so small that it remains unnoticeable for the first dozen iterations, the values diverge completely soon thereafter. This hallmark of chaos is known as *sensitivity to initial conditions*, and it can only happen in *nonlinear* systems; linear update rules like $x_{n+1} = 2x_n + 3$, which transform inputs through simple scaling and shifting, always produce predictable trajectories when defined on the continuous number line.

While repeatedly applying a map is a deterministic process, the term *chaos* suggests unpredictability - so, it is reasonable to ask what is unpredictable about it? Even though it is true that knowing the exact initial values allows one to compute the results, in the real world one never knows the initial conditions to arbitrary precision. Whether it is the weight or the position of an object, there is always some measurement error. This means after a certain point, the behavior of a chaotic system simply cannot be determined, or even approximated.*

* Related to that, there is no simple equation or trick that would allow one to compute, say, x_{100} from x_0. One has basically no choice but to run the numbers through the equation, getting x_1, then x_2, and so on, until reaching x_{100}.

Chaos in the World

The logistic map, while making for an illustrative example of chaos, does not arise from any known physical system. Physical systems, for most practical purposes, are governed by Newton's laws of motion, and they are also sufficient to produce chaotic behavior.

One of the most striking examples of this is the prediction of solar eclipses. Scientists can predict the path and timing of eclipses in the near future very accurately. Assuming there is no cataclysmic event, it seems that predictions should be fairly accurate indefinitely, but that's not the case! According to NASA,[2] the best estimates for the start of eclipse timings for the next 100 years are within a standard deviation of 0.1 seconds. But in about 1,000 years, the standard deviation blows up to as much as 10 minutes. In 5,000 years the uncertainties are matters of many hours, and the eclipse paths are completely unknown.

The uncertainties have multiple causes, but a major reason is that the Earth, the Sun, and the Moon form a three-body system. A system limited to only two celestial objects follows a simple pattern, where both objects take elliptical orbits, as described by the laws of planetary motion formulated in the early seventeenth century by Johannes Kepler.* A small error in the measurement of, say, their positions will propagate as similarly small errors long into the future. What happens, however, when a system has more than two bodies had long eluded scientists, and in the late nineteenth century, King Oscar II of Sweden asked for a solution in a competition. The eminent French mathematician Henri Poincaré became interested in the problem but found it surprisingly difficult to find an exact formula. He observed that in systems of three or more bodies, arbitrarily small measurement errors can cause unpredictable

* Interestingly, the orbital motion of two bodies is not linear in their distance to each other, but it is not chaotic. This illustrates that while nonlinearity is necessary to produce chaos, it is not sufficient.

results. He did not name this phenomenon or develop it as a field, but this is the first documented observation of the phenomenon of sensitivity to initial conditions.

While amusing, predicting eclipses may not seem so significant, but chaos can cause more existential worries. For example, the entire solar system is an n-body, or many-body, system and also subject to chaos. That means that scientists are still not sure whether the current configuration of planets, each nicely orbiting the Sun, is stable in the long term. It is not ruled out that the planets' current neat orbits will eventually degrade into disorder.

Another important application of chaos is of course meteorology, the field that originated Lorenz's butterfly effect. In the 1960s, Lorenz encountered chaos when he wrote down a *dynamical system,* that is, a set of equations that describe change over time.* His system involved three differential equations (equations that describe the rates of change of given quantities) for modeling the phenomenon of warmer air rising and cooler air sinking called atmospheric convection. This phenomenon contributes to everything from cloud formations to thunderstorms, and even tornadoes. His equations became known as the Lorenz system, and he used a computer simulation to model how the system evolves. A visualization of the solutions of the system over time gives the beautiful image in Figure 2.2, which may have even inspired the name the "butterfly effect."

One day, to save time, he restarted the simulation using values that were rounded to less precision than those from his previous run. To his surprise, he discovered that he got completely different results due to the system's sensitivity to initial conditions. It is for this basic reason that weather predictions are virtually impossible after about a week – even with perfect models and extremely precise

* The logistic map described earlier is a special type called a *discrete* dynamical system.

Figure 2.2 Image of the trajectory of the Lorenz system projected to two dimensions for illustration, with the positions taken over time in shades of gray.[3]

measurements, the inherent chaos of atmospheric systems means tiny uncertainties can grow into completely different weather patterns. Unlike Poincaré, Lorenz would devote the rest of his life to studying this phenomenon, and this discovery marked the beginning of the modern study of chaos.

Strange Attractors

Despite the unpredictable nature of chaotic systems, they can also paradoxically exhibit interesting patterns over time. One such example is the trajectory of the Lorenz system illustrated earlier in Figure 2.2; that system appears to follow paths orbiting two distinct loci, forming the familiar butterfly pattern. Individual trajectories never repeat, but over time they remain confined to a geometric set – called an *attractor* – that shapes their long-term behavior. An attractor is a fixed set of states within which all of a system's long-term motion takes place. Although the motion itself never repeats,

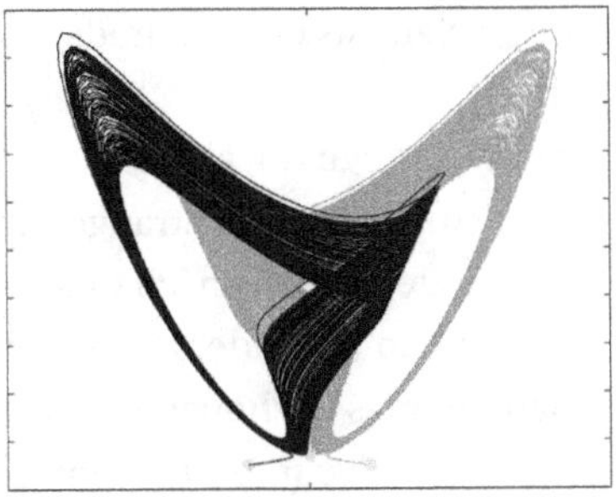

Figure 2.3 Image of a system with two strange attractors, a trajectory around one is in black and around the other in gray.[4]

the attractor has a well-defined shape that the system continually explores.

Many dynamical systems are not chaotic and have simple attractors. A pendulum in the presence of friction will "attract" to the steady state of hanging still. Another example is a grandfather clock with an external energy supply, which regardless of its starting position, enters a repeating cycle. Chaotic systems do not generally settle into steady states or enter repeating cycles, or else their eventual motion would become predictable. But like the Lorenz system, they can still follow unpredictable trajectories around the attractor – such attractors are called *strange*.

A system can also have multiple strange attractors. The trajectories of one such system are depicted in Figure 2.3. This means that once a system enters one attractor, it will stay there in a chaotic orbit. Nudging a trajectory, however, can move it around a different attractor. A potential real-world example of this is in climate modeling. The amount of carbon in the atmosphere is part of a chaotic system. Many climate scientists worry that if too much carbon is released into the atmosphere, the system could be *tipped* from one attractor to a different one. Although there is evidence that Earth's climate has multiple attractors, scientists cannot predict exactly where such tipping points may lie.

It turns out that many, though not all, dynamical systems exhibit strange attractors. The study of these strange attractors is important because they illustrate that even chaotic systems can have predictable patterns that can be understood and sometimes controlled. While the mathematics of showing the existence of strange attractors is too difficult to delve into here, one observation is that most chaotic systems that have strange attractors are dissipative, in that they lose "energy" over time but remain in motion. The Lorenz system for modeling atmospheric convection, for example, continually loses energy through friction and heat dissipation, yet its state traces the butterfly-shaped attractor in Figure 2.2 rather than coming to rest.

Related ideas about exploiting sensitivity to initial conditions and the structure of phase space appear in space mission design, where engineers use chaotic gravitational dynamics that admit multiple long-lived orbital behaviors, toward which trajectories naturally drift. By making small, carefully timed adjustments, a spacecraft can be nudged from one such regime to another, allowing it to reach distant targets using far less fuel than would be required by traditional maneuvers.[6]

A clear illustration of the emergence of structured long-term behavior within chaotic dynamics appears in a simple mathematical setting: the logistic map $x_{n+1} = r\,x_n\,(1 - x_n)$, examined across different values of r, as shown in Figure 2.4. When $r \leq 1$ (a regime not depicted in the figure), no matter what value x_0 starts at, as n goes to infinity, the sequence converges to the steady state of being at 0. Then, for each value of r between $1 < r \leq 3$, there is still one steady state. Then for $3 < r \leq 3.57$, the system repeatedly bifurcates, oscillating among a finite number of values in a repeating cycle. None of these regimes are chaotic. Finally, in the regime

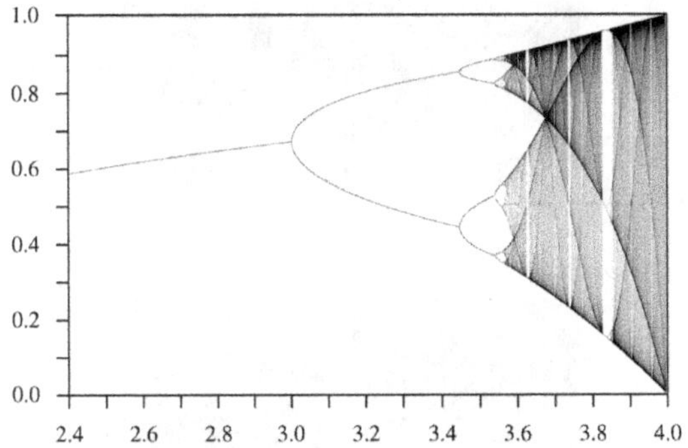

Figure 2.4 A diagram of the logistic map $x_{n+1} = r\, x_n\, (1 - x_n)$ with r values on the x-axis and possible long-term values of x_n on the y-axis.[5]

$3.57 < r < 4$, chaos takes over, and for most values of r in that interval, there is an infinite set of possible values that x_n can take in the long term. However, these values, or states, form a strange attractor, because not all the possible values of x can be arrived at in the long term, irrespective of the starting value of x_0. At $r = 4$ (examined in Figure 2.1), the attractor disappears and the system becomes fully chaotic.

Chaos and Fractals

Another interesting feature of Figure 2.4 is that it exhibits a fractal structure. A *fractal* is a geometric pattern that repeats at different scales, creating complex structures with self-similarity, parts of which resemble the whole structure. Zooming in at $r \approx 3.5$ and $x_n \approx 0.8$, one can see the entire diagram replicated at a smaller scale, with repeated magnifications on the upper branch replicating the bifurcations ad infinitum.

This fractal structure, like most others, arises in part due to the recursive structure of the logistic map, in that to find x_n, one must

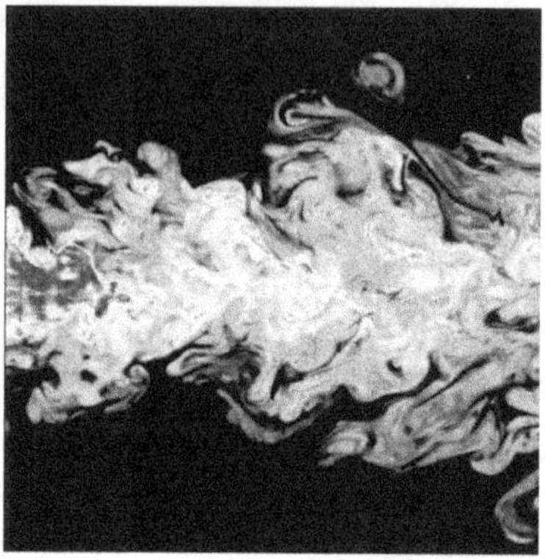

Figure 2.5 A submerged turbulent jet, displayed via laser-induced fluorescence.[7]

compute x_{n-1} using the same formula, which needs the value of x_{n-2} and so on. Fractal structure is, of course, not limited to the logistic map; it also arises from chaotic, and other recursive systems, including in nature. Figure 2.5 shows an image of fractal structure in a turbulent jet, which can be modeled by a famous set of differential equations called Navier–Stokes, which resemble the Lorenz system.

The appearance of fractals in chaotic systems is related to the more general phenomenon of the emergence of complexity from simple rules. Oftentimes, this complexity itself has simplicity, or patterns, within it. And as demonstrated by the logistic map, a complicated system is not needed to produce chaos. Most scientific disciplines, including the ones explored in this book, are replete with such phenomena; these include coastline geometries, the branching of lightning, river systems, and the shape of snowflakes. In this sense, chaos theory shows that complexity and unpredictability are not exceptions but rather pervasive features of science itself.

Further Explorations

Historical Notes

The development of chaos theory emerged from several distinct mathematical and scientific lines of inquiry. Henri Poincaré's late-nineteenth-century analysis of the three-body problem is often cited as the first recognition that deterministic systems can exhibit extreme sensitivity to initial conditions, rendering long-term prediction impossible even in principle.

A rigorous mathematical theory began to take shape in the twentieth century. Early in the century, Aleksandr Lyapunov had introduced a general theory of stability for dynamical systems, including what are now called Lyapunov exponents, which provide a quantitative measure of sensitivity to initial conditions. By the mid 1900s, Andrey Kolmogorov's work on the persistence of quasiperiodic motion under small perturbations, later extended by Vladimir Arnold and Jürgen Moser, clarified the boundary between stable and chaotic dynamics. Around the same time, Stephen Smale introduced a modern framework for hyperbolic dynamical systems, establishing precise mathematical notions of chaos. Together, these developments placed chaos on firm mathematical foundations.

Chaotic behavior was also independently observed in physical systems. In the 1920s, Balthasar van der Pol identified irregular oscillations in nonlinear electrical circuits, and in the 1940s Mary Cartwright and John Littlewood gave a rigorous analysis of such systems, uncovering complex solution structures decades before the term "chaos" came into common use.

Chaos entered the broader scientific consciousness in the 1960s through Edward Lorenz's numerical experiments on atmospheric convection, which revealed sensitive dependence on initial conditions in a remarkably simple model. His discovery helped connect abstract dynamical systems theory to real-world phenomena, particularly in meteorology.

Subsequent work demonstrated the ubiquity of chaotic behavior. Robert May showed that even elementary discrete models, such as the logistic map, can exhibit chaos. Benoît Mandelbrot's study of fractals further revealed the geometric structure underlying many chaotic attractors, building on earlier work by Gaston Julia on the iteration of rational functions. These contributions shaped the modern view of chaos as both mathematically precise and physically pervasive.

For the Mathematically Inclined

The Lorenz system is defined by a set of nonlinear ordinary differential equations. Differential equations define how each variable changes over time as a function of the settings of the other variables. The famous Lorenz system, in which he first observed the butterfly effect, is as follows:

$$\frac{dx}{dt} = \sigma(y - x), \quad \frac{dy}{dt} = x(\rho - z) - y, \quad \frac{dz}{dt} = xy - \beta z.$$

The variables are as follows: $x(t)$ represents the intensity of convective motion, $y(t)$ represents horizontal temperature variation, and $z(t)$ is the vertical temperature variation. The parameters of the system are: σ is the Prandtl number, which is related to fluid viscosity (typically $\sigma = 10$), ρ is the Rayleigh number, which indicates the temperature difference across fluid layers (typically $\rho = 28$), and β is a geometric factor (typically $\beta = \frac{8}{3}$).

These typical parameter values produce the famous Lorenz attractor. Substituting σ=10, ρ=28, and β=8/3 yields the system:

$$\frac{dx}{dt} = 10(y - x), \quad \frac{dy}{dt} = x(28 - z) - y, \quad \frac{dz}{dt} = xy - \frac{8}{3}z.$$

To see the behavior of this system, one must first pick initial values, for example: $x_0 = 1, y_0 = 1, z_0 = 20$. A numerical simulation of the evolution of this system would choose a small time-step, for example, $\Delta t = 0.01$, a number of decimal places to round to, for example, 4, and compute the next values as follows.

First, the derivatives are computed using the Lorenz system equations:

$$\frac{dx}{dt} = 10(y_0 - x_0) = 10(1 - 1) = 0,$$

$$\frac{dy}{dt} = x_0(28 - z_0) - y_0 = 1 \times (28 - 20) - 1 = 7,$$

$$\frac{dz}{dt} = x_0 y_0 - \frac{8}{3} z_0 = 1 \times 1 - \frac{8}{3} \times 20 = -52.3333.$$

Then, substituting in the values and updating by taking the values and adding their derivatives times Δt (this technique is known as Euler's method) results in:

$$x_1 = x_0 + \Delta t \frac{dx}{dt} = 1 + 0.01 \times 0 = 1,$$

$$y_1 = y_0 + \Delta t \frac{dy}{dt} = 1 + 0.01 \times 7 = 1.07,$$

$$z_1 = z_0 + \Delta t \frac{dz}{dt} = 20 + 0.01 \times -52.3333 = 19.4767.$$

Thus, after a timestep of $\Delta t = 0.01$, the values are:*

$$x_1 = 1, \quad y_1 = 1.07, \quad z_1 = 19.4767.$$

Simulations produce a trajectory that moves within the butterfly-shaped Lorenz attractor in Figure 2.2. A small variation in starting

* All quantities computed here are approximate, mainly because the system is updated in small discrete time steps rather than evolving continuously, which inevitably introduces error in any computer simulation. In chaotic systems, these tiny numerical inaccuracies, together with ordinary rounding, can grow rapidly and lead to very different long-term behavior.

values (or time-step values in the simulation), for example setting $x = 1.0001$ instead of 1, leads to drastically different long-term behavior.

Additional Reading

The most acclaimed book on chaos theory is *Chaos: Making a New Science*[8] by the author and science historian James Gleick. In this book he introduced chaos theory to the broader public in the 1980s, and it remains among the most accessible and comprehensive treatments of chaos theory's development. Another excellent book is *Does God Play Dice? The New Mathematics of Chaos*[9] by mathematician Ian Stewart. This book offers some more mathematics and philosophy, as a broader treatment of chaos theory.

3

Hidden Unity
Theory of Relativity

An observer floating in space next to a charged particle will feel an electric field – the influence through which the particle exerts forces on other charges – but not a magnetic one. If the observer moves at a constant velocity relative to the particle, a magnetic field appears. This seems mysterious, because nothing has changed about the particle itself, only the observer's state of motion. This mystery involving electricity and magnetism has a beautiful resolution, and it involves Einstein's theories.

In 1905, the *annus mirabilis* (miraculous year), Albert Einstein published four papers that brought physics into the twentieth century. One of these papers introduced special relativity and became the most famous paper in the history of physics. Another introduced his equation $E = mc^2$, which gave an elegant relationship between mass and energy. This equation reveals that mass and energy are, in a precise sense, interchangeable: Even a tiny amount of mass, when converted, corresponds to an enormous amount of energy. That principle later explained how the Sun shines – through nuclear fusion – and it made possible both nuclear power and nuclear weapons.

Einstein's work seeped into the popular consciousness and revolutionized how space and time are understood, but it also clarified deep connections between previously separate phenomena. In particular, special relativity showed that electric and magnetic fields are not distinct entities but different aspects of a single electromagnetic interaction, depending on the observer's state of motion. Like many of the most profound ideas in physics, relativity reshaped understanding by revealing an underlying unity beneath seemingly unrelated phenomena.

Special Relativity

The special theory of relativity has its origins in a mystery surrounding light. Before quantum theory (discussed in Chapter 5), scientists assumed light was a wave that propagated through an unseen medium called an ether, even though no other evidence for such a medium existed. In 1887, American physicists Albert Michelson and Edward Morley performed a clever experiment to measure the motion of the Earth through this supposed ether. Their idea was to measure the speed of light along two perpendicular paths, with the expectation that the speed of light would differ depending on whether it traveled parallel or perpendicular to Earth's motion through the ether.* In what became "the most famous failed experiment in history,"[10] the speed of light turned

* To do this, Michelson and Morley made use of Michelson's earlier design of a dual-path interferometer. Chapter 5 has a discussion of the basics of interferometry.

out to be the same regardless of whether the light was traveling along the Earth's motion or perpendicular to it.[11] In trying, and failing, to measure the motion of the Earth relative to the ether, Michelson and Morley produced compelling evidence against the existence of the ether in the first place.

The Michelson–Morley experiment demonstrates the importance of a negative result, that is, the result of an experiment that fails to detect or measure the phenomenon it is looking for. Their "failure" not only showed that there probably is no such thing as the ether, but their results also helped motivate Einstein to come up with the idea at the core of relativity. Albert Einstein later remarked, "If the Michelson–Morley experiment had not brought us into serious embarrassment, no one would have regarded the relativity theory as a (halfway) redemption."[12]

Einstein's idea built upon Newton's first law of motion, which states, "An object at rest remains at rest, or if in motion, remains in motion at a constant velocity unless acted on by a net external force." This law describes the behavior of objects in *inertial reference frames*, that is, frames of reference that either remain stationary or move at constant velocity. The special theory of relativity, unlike the more comprehensive and more difficult general theory of relativity, is concerned only with the special case of inertial frames. Motivated in part by the Michelson–Morley result, Einstein postulated that

1. the speed of light in a vacuum is constant in every inertial reference frame, and
2. the laws of physics are the same in every inertial reference frame.

The first assumption does not assign a particular value to the speed of light, but it has been measured to be approximately 299,792,458 meters per second (about 670 million miles per hour) in a vacuum. The second assumption is called "Galilean invariance," which predates even Newton's laws of motion. Galileo imagined a ship that is either still or moving at a constant velocity over a completely

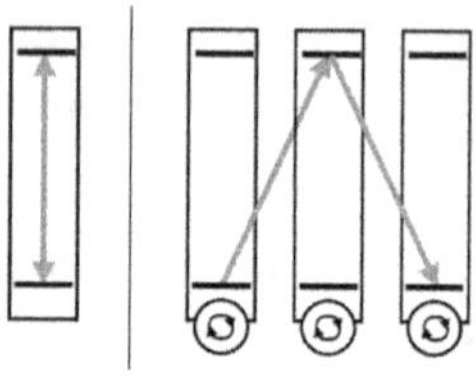

Figure 3.1 On the left is a still light clock. On the right is a moving light clock (each of the three represents a different moment in time).

smooth ocean. He argued that an observer performing experiments below decks, with no access to the outside world, would obtain identical results in either case and therefore could not determine whether the ship was moving or still.[13]

Special relativity follows from these two principles. Relativity has many counterintuitive consequences, including the warping of space and time, the abandonment of the idea that events can happen simultaneously, and the fact that nothing can move faster than the speed of light in a vacuum. People have no intuition for these effects because they only become noticeable at *relativistic speeds*, speeds that are significant fractions of the speed of light. Fortunately, experience with relativistic speeds is not needed to derive relativity's consequences, which can mostly be established from thought experiments. Some of these involve a hypothetical "light clock," where a photon keeps time by bouncing between two mirrors a certain distance apart.

What follows is one such example. On the left side of Figure 3.1, a light clock stands still in an observer's reference frame. On the right side, the same light clock moves rightward, and the light must travel both upward and sideways, following a longer path than in the stationary clock. Because the speed of light must remain the same in both cases, the longer path can only be reconciled if the moving clock ticks more slowly, as measured in the stationary observer's frame. This leads to the phenomenon known as *time dilation*: Time

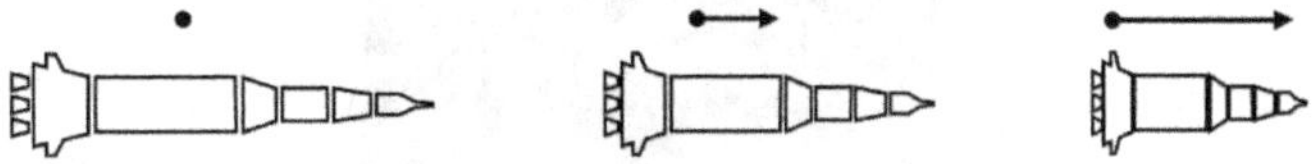

Figure 3.2 A spaceship at rest is depicted on the left, the same spaceship moving is in the center, and the same spaceship moving even faster is on the right. The spaceship's length contracts more in the direction of motion at higher velocities.

runs more slowly in frames moving relative to an observer, and the faster the motion, the greater the required slowing.

Another effect that can be derived from slightly more complicated reasoning is *length contraction.** Objects in a frame moving relative to a stationary observer contract in the direction of motion in the observer's reference frame, and the faster they move, the more they contract in the direction of the motion, as illustrated in Figure 3.2. Importantly, special relativity exhibits a symmetry in the following sense: When one frame moves at constant speed relative to another, either can be considered as the reference frame. From either frame, it is the other frame that experiences time dilation and length contraction. To take the example from Figure 3.2, from the point of view of the reference frame of the spaceship, it is the Earth that is in motion, and, therefore, the object undergoing contraction.

These effects, and others from relativity, have been extensively tested experimentally and confirmed. In the early 1970s, two American scientists – physicist Joseph Hafele and astronomer Richard Keating – performed a dramatic experiment confirming the phenomenon of time dilation. In that experiment, they synchronized two very accurate atomic clocks. They then kept one on the ground and sent the other on an airplane. Upon its return, the clock from

* Length contraction is also called "Lorentz contraction," after the physicist Hendrik Lorentz, who developed the mathematical framework to describe this phenomenon.

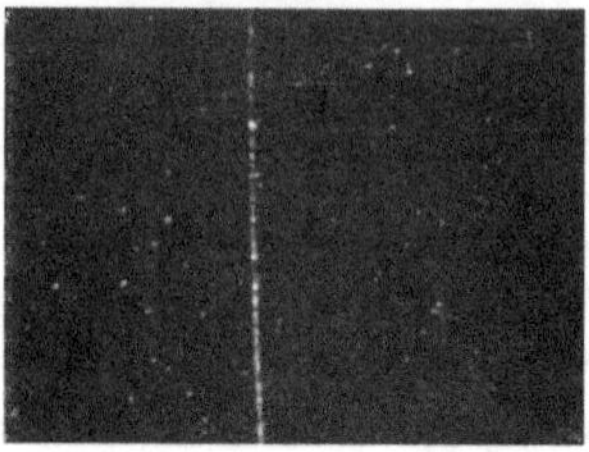

Figure 3.3 Image of a muon that originated from a cosmic ray as it passes through lead in a Wilson cloud chamber (a type of particle detector).[16]

the airplane ran slightly behind.[14] Similarly, satellites orbiting the Earth are subject to time dilation, and the global positioning system (GPS) must correct for it to function properly.*

Cosmic Radiation and Decay

Special relativity helps explain a number of otherwise puzzling phenomena. One striking example is why people can fly in airplanes without being exposed to lethal levels of muon radiation, which consists of fast-moving muons created when cosmic rays strike the upper atmosphere. This example is related to an experiment performed by Italian-American physicist Bruno Rossi and American physicist David Hall, who, in 1940, were the first to experimentally verify time dilation and length contraction.[15]

Coming down from the atmosphere, and traveling at nearly the speed of light, approximately one muon (pictured in Figure 3.3) passes through a person's head every second. Although this constant barrage might sound alarming, it is generally not harmful in such small quantities. Muons are highly unstable

* Technically, GPS systems need corrections from both special and general relativity due to gravitational effects. General relativity is discussed later in this chapter.

particles with a half-life of about 1.5 microseconds. After 1.5 microseconds, a group of 100 muons would decay to approximately 50, and another 1.5 microseconds later, only about 25 would remain, and so on. This decay is so rapid that if every particle in the universe were a muon, they would all vanish within one millisecond.

Muons approach Earth at approximately 1,000 feet per microsecond (this is close to the speed of light). Given that one muon passes through a person's head each second on the Earth's surface, calculations that do not take special relativity into account suggest that at 1,500 feet, two muons should pass through, four at 3,000 feet, and approximately one million (2^{20}) per second at 30,000 feet, a lethal dose after a two-hour flight. These calculations are clearly wrong since aircraft routinely fly at 30,000 feet without subjecting passengers to lethal radiation.

The discrepancy can be explained by examining the relativistic effects experienced by the muons as a result of their high velocity. For an observer on Earth, muons decay about 10 times more slowly than their actual half-life because of time dilation. Consequently, instead of experiencing 20 halvings, observers perceive only two. Thus, at 30,000 feet, only about 4 muons per second pass through a person's head, a nonlethal amount.

Conversely, from the muons' reference frame, it is the observers' clocks that slow down, not their own. From that perspective, the muons only go through two halvings due to the length contraction. From their reference frame, muons halve only twice between airplane height and the Earth's surface because, to them, the traversed distance is 3,000 feet, not 30,000, so they are able to cover it much faster.

This example highlights how special relativity reshapes familiar ideas of time and distance without introducing any new forces. Electricity and magnetism provide the next piece of the story.

Electricity and Magnetism

From prehistoric observations of lightning to the Han dynasty's use of lodestones as compasses in the third century BCE, people have long been familiar with the phenomena of electricity and magnetism. Although the ancients were unaware of it, these forces are omnipresent: When two objects collide, it is electromagnetic forces that repel them from one another.

The *electrical force* is a force of attraction or repulsion between charged particles. Charges are either positive or negative. If the charges have opposite signs, the electrical force is attractive. If they are of the same sign (both positive or negative), the electrical force is repulsive. Coulomb's law states that the strength of the electrical force is proportional to the product of the magnitude of the charges and inversely proportional to the square of the distance between them.[17]* It is the Coulomb force that keeps distinct objects from going through each other; when the distance becomes small enough, the electrons orbiting the atoms of one object repel those of the other. Another concept involving electric charge is *electrical current*, which is the flow of electric charge through a wire or some other conductor.

The *magnetic force* is exerted by a magnet onto another magnetic material or onto a moving electric charge or current. The magnetic force between two magnetic poles can also be attractive or repulsive depending on whether their polarity matches, and like the electrical force, it becomes weaker with distance. The magnetic force on a moving electric charge or current is always *perpendicular* to both the velocity of the charged particle or current and the direction of the magnetic field. At the beginning of the twentieth century,

* Coulomb's law gives the magnitude of the force, $F = k_e \frac{|q_1 q_2|}{r^2}$, where k_e is a constant (known as Coulomb's constant), q_1 and q_2 are the magnitudes of the charges, and r is the distance between the particles.

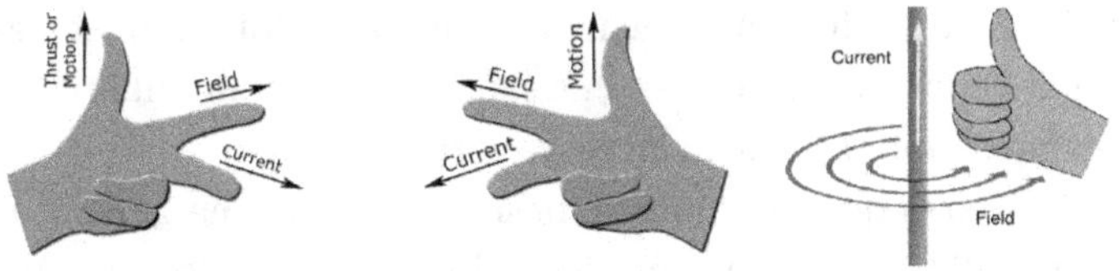

(a) Fleming's left-hand rule for determining the direction of force acting on a current-carrying conductor in a magnetic field.[18]

(b) Fleming's right-hand rule for determining the direction of induced current from movement through a magnetic field.[19]

(c) Ampère's right-hand grip rule for determining the direction of a magnetic field induced by a current.[20]

Figure 3.4 The *left-hand rule*, the *right-hand rule*, and the *right-hand grip rule.*

the British electrical engineer John Fleming introduced the "left-hand rule" to quickly determine the direction of a magnetic force on a current (shown in Figure 3.4a) and the "right-hand rule" to quickly determine the direction of an induced current in a magnetic field (shown in Figure 3.4b).[21] For visualizing the direction of a magnetic field induced by a current, Ampère's right-hand grip rule is used (shown in Figure 3.4c). These rules have been helping (and sometimes confusing) students of physics for more than a century.

The relationship between electricity and magnetism is captured by a set of equations developed by the great Scottish physicist James Clerk Maxwell, which by the 1870s unified previously known electromagnetic phenomena.[22]* One of these is a generalization of Ampère's law, which states that electric currents generate magnetic fields.[23] Another is Faraday's Law, which states that a changing magnetic field induces an electric field.[24] Modern generators

* These equations also describe light as an electromagnetic wave. Chapter 5 has more detail on the "dual nature" of light and other particles.

produce electricity from mechanical motion in this manner – as a simplification of this process, one can imagine a windmill spinning a magnet around a wire to induce a current within it.

Maxwell's equations unified these phenomena mathematically, but they did not explain why electricity and magnetism should be so closely linked. That deeper connection emerges only when the description of electromagnetic fields is examined from different states of motion.

Unification of the Forces

In his original paper, Einstein pointed out that special relativity offers a new way to think about electricity and magnetism. The connection between these two seemingly distinct forces turns out to be surprisingly deep. A simple example shows how.

The setup involves two parallel wires, each carrying a current in the same direction. To simplify matters, one can consider the electrons as the charges in motion, while the protons remain stationary. Although it is the electrons that move, the direction of the current is defined by convention as the direction in which positive charges (the protons) would move, opposite to the electrons' motion.

According to Ampère's law, each wire produces a magnetic field circling around the wire, as given by the right-hand grip rule, which is applied using the direction of the current. These magnetic fields are illustrated in Figure 3.5. In experiments conducted by Ampère, when current runs in the same direction along two parallel wires, they attract each other. Fleming's left-hand rule is consistent with this experimental result. When the current in the bottom wire points to the left (corresponding to electrons moving to the right), and the magnetic field produced by the top wire points into the page, the resulting force is upward, toward the other wire. The top

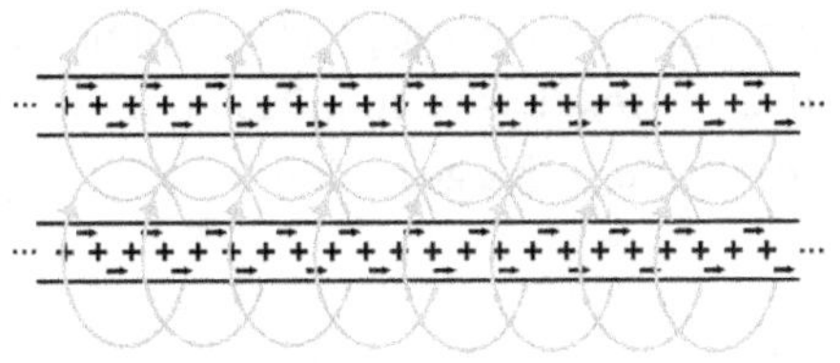

Figure 3.5 An illustration of current in two parallel wires, each inducing a magnetic field. The plus signs show the protons, the minus signs with arrows show the moving electrons drifting rightward, and the magnetic field is shown in gray. The current in both wires flows *leftward* (⟵), opposite the direction of the electrons.

wire behaves analogously and is pushed downward, toward the bottom wire.

But it is also possible to understand this magnetic effect as a relativistic consequence of the electric force. For simplicity, it is convenient to assume that the wires are infinitely long. The electrons in both wires move in the reference frame of the stationary protons. Because of length contraction, the moving electrons are contracted along the direction of motion, leading to a higher linear charge density. This increased charge density results in a net attractive electric force on the stationary protons in the other wire. Similarly, in the reference frame of the electrons, the protons move and are length-contracted, leading again to a higher charge density and the same net attractive force. In any reference frame, the net physical result is the same.

To determine the magnitude of the attractive force using traditional methods, Ampère's law requires the strength of the current. The current can be expressed in terms of the electron drift velocity and charge density, which are sufficient for the relevant relativistic calculations. When the magnitude of the attractive electric force is computed using relativistic length contraction, it agrees exactly with the magnetic force calculated using Ampère's law.

This example illustrates a deep connection: Magnetism can be understood as a relativistic manifestation of electric forces acting between moving charges. That is an insight worthy of Einstein!

General Relativity

The special theory of relativity changed the way physicists thought about time and motion and illustrated a profound connection between electricity and magnetism, but it was limited to the case of inertial reference frames. Einstein spent another decade wrestling with this limitation, seeking to develop a theory that could encompass all motion, including acceleration. His final theory, the *general theory of relativity*, was a triumph of modern physics that led to another unexpected unification – this time between gravity and acceleration – and to concrete predictions, including the bending of light by gravity and measurable distortions of time near massive objects.[25]

Just as the special theory of relativity began with a thought experiment about observing a moving clock (as illustrated in Figure 3.1), the general theory also begins with a thought experiment. Einstein imagined being inside a freely falling elevator; in such a scenario, gravity would appear to vanish, and all objects would float weightlessly together. This is because all objects inside the elevator, including any observers, are accelerating at the same rate due to gravity, creating the sensation of weightlessness.

He realized that one cannot distinguish between being in free fall and being in deep space where gravity is absent. Similarly, being in an accelerating elevator feels identical to experiencing a gravitational field: An observer in an elevator accelerating upward in empty space feels pressed to the floor in exactly the same way as an observer standing still on the Earth.

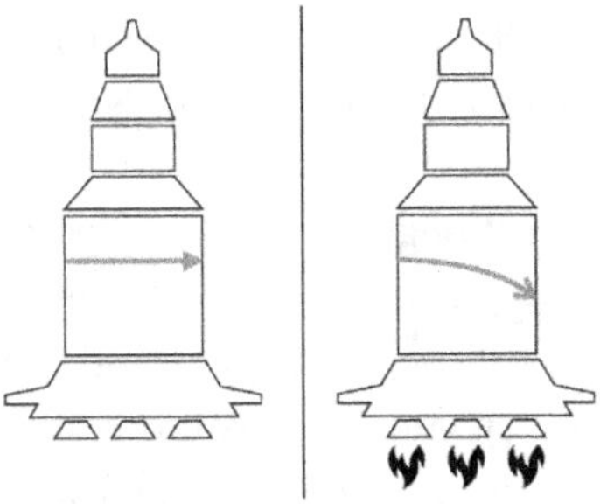

Figure 3.6 On the left is a beam of light travelling horizontally in a non-accelerating spaceship in deep space. On the right is the trajectory of the same beam of light in a spaceship experiencing acceleration upward.

This insight led Einstein to formulate a new principle of relativity called the *equivalence principle*: The effects of a locally uniform gravitational field are locally indistinguishable from the effects of uniform acceleration.* One implication is that no local experiment can tell whether an observer is at rest in a gravitational field or accelerating in the absence of gravity.

Applying the equivalence principle led Einstein to a profound conclusion. Figure 3.6 illustrates the idea. In an inertial frame, a beam of light traveling horizontally across a spaceship follows a straight-line path. Yet when the spaceship accelerates upward, an observer inside the spaceship sees the light follow a curved, downward path relative to the ship. Such an observer would also feel a constant "gravitational pull" toward the floor. By the equivalence principle, this accelerating spaceship is locally indistinguishable from a stationary spaceship in a gravitational field, such as an elevator at rest on Earth. Therefore, if light appears to bend for

* The "local" condition means that the principle only holds within a sufficiently small region of space and time. For example, in a large falling elevator, objects at the top and bottom would accelerate slightly differently in the Earth's gravitational field. This point is rather subtle and therefore omitted in the present discussion.

observers in an accelerating spaceship, it must also appear to bend in a gravitational field. In other words, gravity affects the path of light!

Einstein's elevator thought experiment led to more than a new way of thinking about gravity – it led to a deeper synthesis. Special relativity had already shown that space and time are intertwined, with motion stretching time and compressing length. Together, space and time form a single entity, called *spacetime.* Events that appear separated in space to one observer may be separated in time to another, reflecting the fact that space and time are inseparable aspects of a single structure. General relativity carried this insight further, showing that spacetime need not be flat but can be curved. It is the curvature of spacetime, shaped by mass and energy, that gives rise to the effects known as gravity.

Viewed this way, gravity is no longer something that acts from one object to another across space. Instead, mass and energy influence the shape of spacetime around them, and that shape determines how objects move. This shift, from describing interactions as forces to describing them as consequences of geometry, has shaped much of modern physics.

Further Explorations

Historical Notes

Practical applications of electricity and magnetism go back to the Ancient Greeks and Ancient Chinese, who discovered the first uses of magnets, including for compasses. In the seventeenth century, Otto von Guericke invented the electrostatic generator. In the eighteenth century, Ewald Georg von Kleist and Pieter van Musschenbroek independently invented the Leyden jar, a precursor to the battery. In the nineteenth century, Michael Faraday developed the first electric generator (employing the induction method discussed earlier). Many other advanced developments followed.

The theoretical understanding of electricity goes back to Charles-Augustin de Coulomb, who formulated his law in the late eighteenth century. In the nineteenth century, André-Marie Ampère, Michael Faraday, and others, including Carl Friedrich Gauss, Joseph Henry, and Georg Simon Ohm, set the foundations of electromagnetism. Important contributions were also made by Henry Cavendish, whose unpublished work anticipated many of Coulomb's results, by Hans Christian Ørsted, who first demonstrated a direct connection between electricity and magnetism, and by Heinrich Hertz, who experimentally confirmed the existence of electromagnetic waves.

These efforts culminated in James Clerk Maxwell's theory unifying electricity and magnetism into a single mathematical framework. Maxwell's equations do far more than describe electric and magnetic fields: They underpin essentially all modern electrical and communication technologies, from power generation and electric motors to radio, radar, and wireless communication, and they even predicted the existence of electromagnetic waves – light itself. Maxwell's laws are not nearly as famous as Einstein's equation $E = mc^2$, but they still appear all over the world on plaques, mugs, and shirts.

In 1905, Albert Einstein published his paper on special relativity and made the central insight of this chapter that magnetism is simply a relativistic effect of electricity and that they are the same force. His famous equation $E = mc^2$ is also a consequence of special relativity and was published in a follow-up paper that same year. Einstein built upon earlier work by Hendrik Lorentz, who independently developed the mathematical transformations that bear his name and won the Nobel Prize for other contributions to physics. In the middle of the twentieth century, Richard Feynman, Julian Schwinger, and Shin'ichirō Tomonaga shared the Nobel for developing a quantum theory of electromagnetism called QED, for quantum electrodynamics.

General relativity received experimental confirmation in 1919, when Arthur Eddington observed the bending of starlight around the Sun during a total solar eclipse. Further confirmation came from explaining the anomalous orbit of Mercury, which had puzzled astronomers for decades. The mathematics produced by this theory even predicted the existence of black holes, objects so massive that even light cannot escape them. Even Einstein initially doubted their existence; yet, these too were eventually discovered and confirmed.

For the Mathematically Inclined

It is possible to derive some of the basic equations of special relativity without much difficulty. In Figure 3.1, the distances can be labeled as follows. The separation between the two mirrors is denoted by L. The length of the diagonal path followed by the light in the moving clock between successive reflections will be denoted by D. As usual, c denotes the speed of light.

In the rest frame of the clock, the time required for the light to travel up and back is $t = 2L/c$. In the frame in which the clock is moving, the corresponding time is $t' = 2D/c$, where t' denotes the time measured in the moving frame.

During this interval, the clock moves horizontally at speed v, covering a total distance vt'. Half of this distance is traversed during each leg of the light's journey, forming a right triangle whose diagonal has length D, vertical side has length L, and horizontal side has length $vt'/2$. By the Pythagorean theorem, this triangle satisfies $D^2 = L^2 + (vt'/2)^2$, and hence $D = \sqrt{L^2 + (vt'/2)^2}$.

Substituting this expression for D into the relation $t' = 2D/c$ and using the relation $t = 2L/c$ yields what is known as the *time dilation*

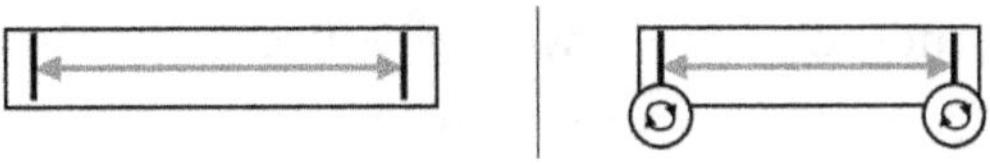

Figure 3.7 On the left is a stationary light clock. On the right is the same light clock moving horizontally.

equation, $t' = \gamma(v)\,t$, where $\gamma(v)$ is called the *Lorentz factor* and is defined as

$$\gamma(v) = 1/\sqrt{1 - \frac{v^2}{c^2}}.$$

A different thought experiment is useful for determining the amount of length contraction. In this case, the light clock is oriented horizontally so that the light travels along the direction of motion, as shown in Figure 3.7.

Once again, L denotes the length of the clock in its rest frame, and the round-trip time for the light is $t = 2L/c$. In the observer's frame, the moving clock has a contracted length L'. The light always travels at speed c in every frame.

During the forward leg of the journey, the front of the clock moves away from the light at speed v. If t_1' denotes the time for this leg, then by the time the light reaches the front mirror, that mirror has moved a distance vt_1', so the light travels a total distance $L' + vt_1'$. Since the light travels at speed c, this distance satisfies $ct_1' = L' + vt_1'$. Similarly, during the return leg, the back of the clock moves toward the light at speed v. If t_2' denotes the time for the return journey, the light travels a distance $L' - vt_2'$, and hence $ct_2' = L' - vt_2'$. Solving these equations gives $t_1' = L'/(c-v)$ and $t_2' = L'/(c+v)$, so the total round-trip time is $t' = t_1' + t_2' = \frac{L'}{c-v} + \frac{L'}{c+v}$.

Combining this expression for t' with the time dilation relation derived above yields the *length contraction equation*, $L' = L/\gamma(v)$.

As a check, indeed $\gamma(v) = 1$ when $v = 0$, and $\gamma(v)$ grows without bound as v approaches the speed of light c.

Additional Reading

The book *Why Does E = mc²? (And Why Should We Care?)*[26] by Brian Cox and Jeff Forshaw gives more detailed explanations of relativity and its relationship to electricity and magnetism. Also worth reading is *Relativity: The Special and the General Theory,*[27] in which Albert Einstein attempts to explain relativity to a non-specialist audience. Einstein's book requires some mathematical sophistication.

4

Machines and Minds Computation, Complexity, and AI

From the first appearance of computers, programmers have had to adapt their thinking to make effective use of them. More broadly, computers have reshaped how people reason across many domains, from scientific modeling and economic forecasting to creative design. As Dutch computing pioneer Edsger Dijkstra observed, "The tools we use have a profound and devious influence on our thinking habits, and therefore on our thinking abilities."[28]

These changes naturally invite deeper questions. Can machines be programmed to think like people? Can they exhibit intelligence, or even consciousness? While such questions are often framed philosophically, advances in computer science have revealed that they hinge on deeper structural facts about computation itself: which tasks can be carried out at all, which can be performed efficiently, and how computational limitations can sometimes be exploited rather than merely endured. These ideas lie at the heart of computational complexity, cryptography, and the modern study of machine intelligence.

The Decision Problem

In 1900, the eminent German mathematician David Hilbert compiled a list of 23 problems that set the research agenda for twentieth-century mathematics.[29] The second problem on this list had the seed of an idea that eventually inspired Alan Turing to establish the foundations of an entirely new field now called computer science. Hilbert's second problem asked for a proof that the *Peano axioms*, which form the foundations of arithmetic, are mutually consistent – that is, that they do not lead to any internal contradictions. Later, as part of the same program to formalize mathematics, Hilbert and his colleague Wilhelm Ackermann asked (using current terminology) for an *algorithm*, or procedure, that, given a set of mathematical axioms, would tell whether a statement has a proof.[30] This became known as the *Entscheidungsproblem*, which translates to "the decision problem" from German.

Hilbert's second problem was eventually tackled by Kurt Gödel in 1931, who famously showed that it is impossible to prove that the Peano axioms are consistent within Peano arithmetic itself.[31] Hilbert and Ackermann's Entscheidungsproblem was similarly resolved in 1936 by Alan Turing, who reframed the question in computational terms by introducing a theoretical model of computation and proving that it would be impossible to answer certain questions about it.[32]

Turing's model, now called a *universal Turing machine* (UTM), was not intended as a physical device but as an abstract representation of what it means to carry out a mechanical procedure. Its details are unimportant for the present discussion. What is important is

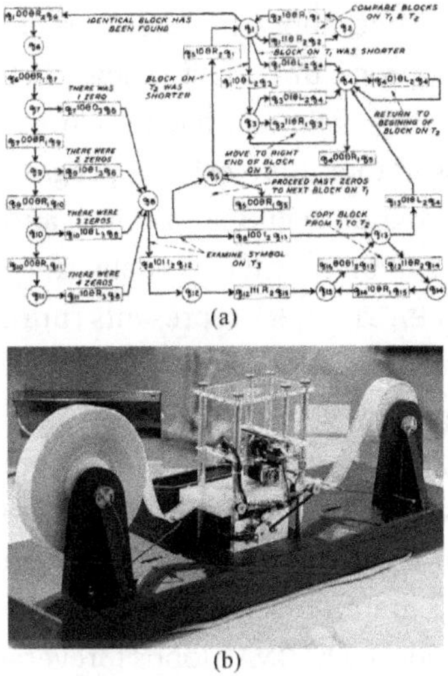

Figure 4.1 (a) A UTM diagram by E. F. Moore, a mathematical depiction[33] and (b) a physical realization of a UTM.[34]

that any well-formed algorithm could be implemented on Turing's abstract universal device (shown in Figure 4.1a). One can even build a physical version (as in Figure 4.1b).* This universality allows questions about computation to be separated from the mechanics of any particular machine. Rather than focusing on how a computation is carried out, it is sufficient to think in terms of ordinary algorithms or programs written abstractly, knowing that any such procedure could be carried out by a Turing machine.

With this framework in place, Turing turned to a single, carefully chosen problem that captures the heart of Hilbert's question: the

* Turing's model does require Turing machines to have an infinite amount of "tape" for memory storage. Of course, their various physical embodiments had to have a limited amount of tape, just as real-world computers have a limited amount of memory.

halting problem. If one hopes to determine, in general, whether a statement has a proof, one must at least be able to determine whether a given computational procedure ever finishes its work at all. Turing supposed that there exists a program called `HALT` that takes as input a program `P` and an input `S`, and correctly predicts whether `P`, when run on `S`, will eventually stop or instead run forever. The notation `HALT(P,S)` represents running `HALT` on `P` and `S`. It should return `true` for those programs that stop and `false` for those that loop forever.

If `HALT` exists, one can also create a program `DIAGONAL` as in Algorithm 4.2 that takes in program `P` and checks whether `P` will ever stop when run *on its own code*. The ingenious idea here is to use the code of the program `P` itself as the second input to `HALT`. If `P` stops on its own code, `DIAGONAL` loops forever; whereas, if `P` loops forever when run on its own code, `DIAGONAL` stops.*

```
program DIAGONAL(P):
    if HALT(P,P)=true, then
        loop forever
    else
        stop program
end program
```

Algorithm 4.2: `DIAGONAL(P)`.

Now, what happens if one runs `DIAGONAL(DIAGONAL)`, that is, runs `DIAGONAL` on its own code? If `HALT` says that `DIAGONAL` is supposed to stop, then `DIAGONAL` runs forever, and if `HALT` says `DIAGONAL` is supposed to run forever, then `DIAGONAL` stops. This "proof by contradiction" implies that the `HALT` program could not have existed in the first place. In this way, Turing showed that

* The program is so named because this technique is a variant of Cantor's "diagonalization argument" for showing there are more real numbers than integers.[35]

even though deciding whether a program ever stops running on a given piece of code is well-defined, there is no general way to tell!* Hilbert's hope for a universal decision procedure was thereby extinguished.

Turing's design of an unsolvable problem already required an element of *computational thinking* – reasoning about problems in the way a computer could solve them. This approach revealed something even more profound: His insight, known as the *Church–Turing thesis*, postulated that Turing machines capture all forms of computation, whether done by humans or machines. Even someone who wants to solve a problem without a computer (like Turing solving the Entscheidungsproblem) can benefit from thinking about how computers solve problems.

This result revealed a fundamental limitation of computation itself. The halting problem was not an isolated curiosity but the first example of a vast class of undecidable problems. Over time, researchers discovered that many natural questions one would like to ask about programs – whether they terminate, whether they always produce correct output, whether they satisfy a given specification, or whether they exhibit particular behaviors – cannot be answered by any algorithm, even in principle.

A particularly sweeping result, proved by the American logician Henry Rice in 1951, makes this limitation precise. Rice's theorem shows that there is no general procedure for determining any nontrivial semantic property of a program solely from its code.[36] In other words, once a property depends on what a program actually does, no algorithm can decide it in all cases.

This result has some immediate consequences across computing. It implies, for example, that there can never be a perfect virus scanner, meaning that the arms race between malware creators

* It is tempting to solve this problem by running the program to see if it ever stops. The problem then becomes when to "give up" on it ever stopping if it runs for a very long time.

and security system designers is likely to continue indefinitely. For the same reason, no tool will be able to perfectly predict whether a piece of software will function as intended by its designers. More broadly, Rice's theorem exemplifies a broader phenomenon about sufficiently rich systems. When models become expressive enough to encode computation, questions about their behavior become provably undecidable. These include many biological models, physical systems, and even frameworks for legal reasoning.

Computational Efficiency

Turing's discovery of the universal machine seemed to answer the most foundational questions involving the theoretical understanding of computers. There was, of course, the issue of building real-world machines and programming them, but both seemed to be more engineering challenges. The new and even more applicable theoretical questions only came about later, after Turing's tragic death in 1954, when notions of *efficiency*, which concern the resources required to carry out a computation rather than mere solvability, became central to understanding what problems can be solved.

This reorientation of theoretical computer science was initiated in 1965 by a foundational paper by the American computing pioneers Juris Hartmanis and Richard Stearns in which they established the field of *computational complexity*.[37] Hartmanis and Stearns convincingly argued that the divide between solvable problems and unsolvable ones fails to take into account problems that are solvable but take a long time. As the economist John Maynard Keynes famously wrote, "In the long run, we are all dead."[38] Around the same time, the now-standard dividing line of polynomial time was proposed independently by computer

Table 4.3 Comparison of n^2 and $n!$ for increasing values of n.

n	n^2	$n!$
3	9	6
10	100	3,628,800
100	10,000	$\approx 9.33 \times 10^{157}$

scientists Alan Cobham,[39] Jack Edmonds,[40] and Michael Rabin[41] as a way to capture those problems that can be solved efficiently.

An example may help illustrate the notion of polynomial time. The problem of finding the closest pair among a set of n points can be solved by checking all distances between distinct pairs of points, of which there are approximately n^2. The resulting number of computational steps therefore grows like the polynomial n^2. Conversely, if some problem requires trying all permutations, or orderings, of n numbers to solve, that would behave as $n!$,* which grows faster than any polynomial. Table 4.3 gives the values of n^2 and $n!$ for different values of n. The entry for 100! is inordinately bigger than the best estimate of the number of atoms in the universe.[42] Polynomials tend to stay within reasonable limits, whereas faster growing functions, like factorial, tend to quickly get out of control.

It is not at all straightforward to tell which problems are polynomial-time solvable and which are not. Many problems appear to require an exponential amount of work but have clever solutions that allow for efficient algorithms. To give a simple example: There are $n!$ orderings of n numbers, but to sort n numbers, it would be wasteful to try all the possible orderings until the right one is found. Instead, repeatedly pulling out the smallest remaining

* The ! symbol here stands for factorial, where $n! = n \times (n-1) \times (n-2) \times \cdots \times 1$.

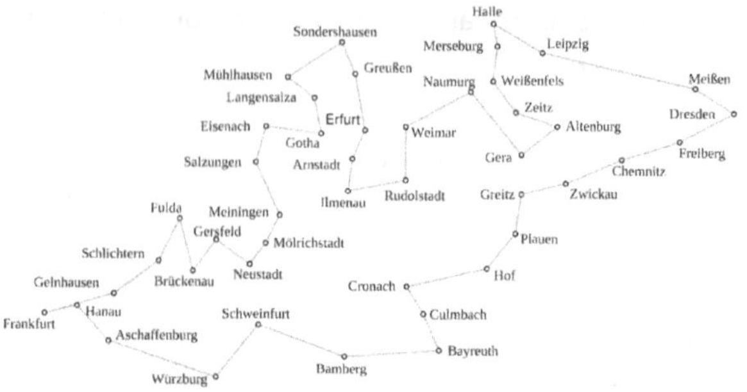

Figure 4.4 Visualization of a proposed route for visiting German cities from an 1832 book for traveling salesmen.[43] No mathematical guarantees were given.[44]

number until all are sorted takes roughly n^2 steps.* The problem of sorting illustrates how a problem with an enormous space of possible solutions can nonetheless admit an efficient algorithm.

The next breakthrough in complexity theory came in the early 1970s, when American-Canadian mathematician Stephen Cook, and separately the then Soviet mathematician Leonid Levin, formulated the P versus NP problem. This problem asks whether every computational problem whose solutions can be efficiently checked can also be efficiently solved. The class NP consists of computational problems with the property that, whenever a proposed solution is given, there exists an efficient procedure for checking whether that solution is correct.† The class P, by contrast, consists of those problems for which an efficient algorithm is known that directly computes a solution.

As a concrete example, the *traveling salesman problem* (TSP), illustrated in Figure 4.4, is defined as follows. Given a set of cities

* There are faster ways to sort, but this approach is sufficient for the present discussion.

† This highlights the importance of NP problems, since a solution that cannot be efficiently verified is of limited practical use.

and a distance budget, the problem asks whether there exists a route that visits each city exactly once while staying within the allotted total distance. If a candidate route is provided, checking that it visits all cities and satisfies the distance constraint is straightforward, which places TSP in NP. No algorithm is currently known that can efficiently determine such a route from scratch, however, so TSP is not known to lie in P.

In the course of their work, Cook and Levin independently identified a remarkable subclass of NP problems, now known as NP-complete problems. These problems have the defining property that an efficient solution to any one of them would yield efficient solutions to all problems in NP. In this sense, they capture the intrinsic difficulty of the entire class. Shortly thereafter, American computer scientist Richard Karp showed that a wide range of fundamental problems, including the traveling salesman problem, are NP-complete.[45] As a result, an efficient algorithm for TSP would imply that P equals NP.

The status of the P versus NP question has far-reaching implications. Many scientifically important problems fall into NP. One example arises in protein folding, where the task is to determine the three-dimensional structure of a protein from its amino acid sequence. Given a proposed folding, its validity can often be checked efficiently, but no general efficient algorithm is known for computing the correct folding itself. If P were equal to NP, such structures could in principle be computed efficiently, dramatically accelerating biological research and drug discovery (illustrated in Figure 4.5).

Another philosophically interesting application is the production of mathematical proofs. Most competent mathematicians can verify a mathematical proof, but there is no known procedure to efficiently produce one. If P = NP, then mathematical proofs would, in some sense, be as easy to produce algorithmically as to verify. Currently, mathematics is considered a highly creative endeavor,

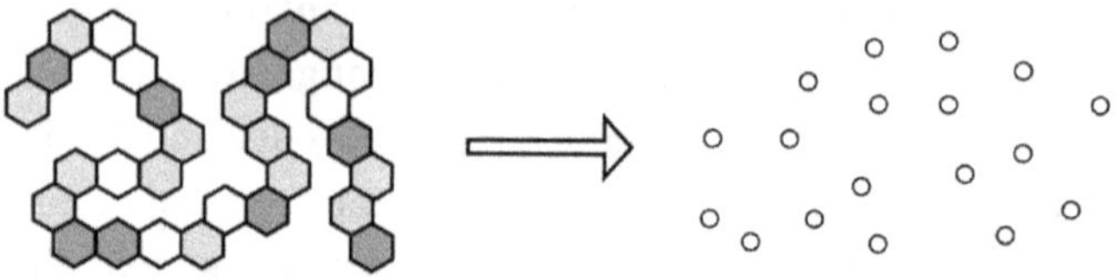

Figure 4.5 On the left is an illustration of an amino acid sequence. On the right is an illustration of a set of cities to tour. Each protein-folding instance (and also any instance of any other problem in NP) can be turned into an instance of the traveling salesman problem (or of any other NP-complete problem). Finding the optimal traveling salesman tour on this transformed problem would solve the original protein-folding problem. This is guaranteed by the Cook–Levin theorem.

but if P = NP, it could be efficiently automated, at least in principle. This seems very unlikely, and indeed, most mathematicians believe that P $\neq$ NP, and not just because they want to stay employed. In fact, conjectures related to the status of the P versus NP problem can be used to explain phenomena in physics, demonstrating an intricate link between computational and physical phenomena.[46] Despite these considerations, no proof is known either way, and whether P equals NP remains the most famous open problem in computer science.

Shared Secrets

One striking consequence of the P versus NP problem is that computational hardness can serve as a resource rather than merely an obstacle. Modern cryptography relies on a closely related kind of asymmetry: Certain operations are easy to carry out but appear computationally infeasible to reverse. The following example illustrates a surprising way in which the presumed existence of such hardness can be put to use.

Imagine three people, Alice, Bob, and Eve, all strangers, walking into a room and meeting for the first time. Alice and Bob want some privacy from Eve, "the eavesdropper," but unfortunately for them, she can hear everything they say to each other.* Is it possible for Alice and Bob to come up with a shared secret that Eve does not know? To most who first hear about the problem, it seems an impossible task, but an astounding insight from cryptography shows that it is actually possible!†

In 1976, American cryptographers Whitfield Diffie and Martin Hellman published an ingenious solution to this problem, now known as the Diffie–Hellman key exchange.[47] The central idea is to exploit an asymmetry between operations that are easy to perform and those that are difficult to undo. Alice and Bob publicly agree on a simple computational procedure and then each add their own private input. Although the resulting messages are exchanged openly, combining them in the right way allows Alice and Bob to arrive at the same shared secret. An eavesdropper, by contrast, would have to reverse the underlying operation in order to recover the secret, a task believed to require an infeasible amount of computation.

In practice, this asymmetry is provided by special computational tasks known as *one-way functions*: operations that are easy to carry out but believed to be difficult to reverse – such functions can only exist if P is not equal to NP. Alice and Bob rely only on efficient computations and public communication, while Eve's only option is to attempt a prohibitively expensive computation, even after observing everything that is said. This idea is illustrated with an analogy involving paint in Figure 4.6.

* No cheating is allowed. Alice and Bob are not allowed to secretly write to each other, they do not know a shared foreign language, etc.

† Once they have a shared secret, they can use it as a "private key" to encrypt their conversation. Going into details of how this is done is beyond the scope of this chapter.

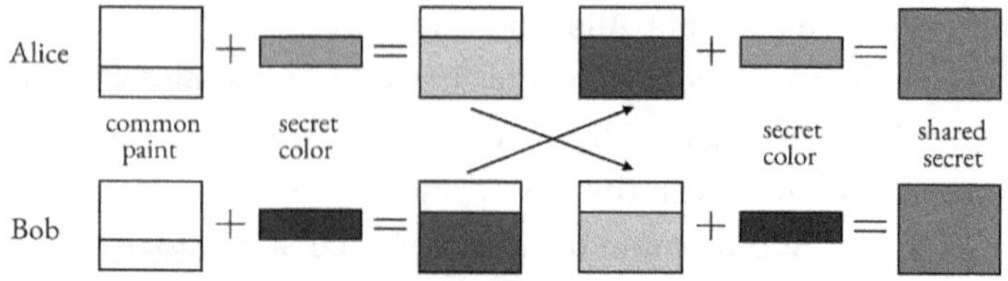

Figure 4.6 The Diffie–Hellman key exchange illustrated with paints. Assume paint is easy to mix but hard to unmix. First, Alice and Bob publicly agree to a common paint. Then, they each invent their own secret color. Next, they each mix their own secret color with the common paint and send each other the result. Finally, they each add their own secret paint to the paint they received. Their shared secret is the common paint + Alice's secret color + Bob's secret color. Eve can see what is sent and the common paint but cannot reproduce the shared secret without unmixing.

Cryptography shows that the limits of efficient computation are not merely theoretical curiosities but have concrete consequences for what machines can and cannot do. In some cases, these limits can be harnessed to provide security; in others, they constrain the extent to which human tasks can be mechanized. The boundary between what computation enables and what it resists becomes especially significant when machines are programmed to emulate aspects of human intelligence.

Thinking Machines

In his seminal paper that is often credited with launching the field of *artificial intelligence,* which is concerned with programming computers to perform tasks traditionally associated with human intelligence, Turing introduced the "imitation game." In this game, a person tries to tell whether he is talking to a computer or another person. In 1950, Turing wrote "I believe that in about fifty years' time it will be possible to programme computers, with a storage capacity of about 10^9 [approximately 100 MB] to make them play the imitation game so well that an average interrogator will not have more than 70 percent chance of making the right identification after five minutes of questioning."[48] Turing proposed the imitation game to avoid philosophical debates about what intelligence is. His argument was that since humans are considered intelligent, the imitation game can be used as a test of intelligence for machines. This test became known as the *Turing test*.

Turing's time frame arguably turned out to be not too far off. Though the test has not fully resolved debates about the nature of intelligence, technologies like `ChatGPT` can arguably pass the Turing test.[49] `ChatGPT` uses more memory than the 100 megabytes estimate by Turing, but algorithms using less memory can also do a decent job on the test, so even this estimate is not unreasonable. But the way Turing imagined it coming about was unrealistic: In that same article, he speculated that "sixty workers, working steadily through the fifty years might accomplish the job."

In fact, the first attempts at building artificially intelligent systems employed the "rule-based" approach suggested by Turing. Computer scientists tried to explicitly program rules and logic into the system code. The complexity of the programming tasks, coupled with the inability of programmers to predict all possible scenarios in advance, led largely to failure. That time, which spanned from about 1970 until the early 2000s, led to periods often referred to as "AI winters," during which optimism and funding sharply declined. Though there were some partial successes, especially in the early to mid 1980s, optimism and funding for artificial intelligence were generally in short supply.

An important insight that helped get the field of artificial intelligence out of these winters came from the related field of *machine learning*. Machine learning algorithms, unlike traditional

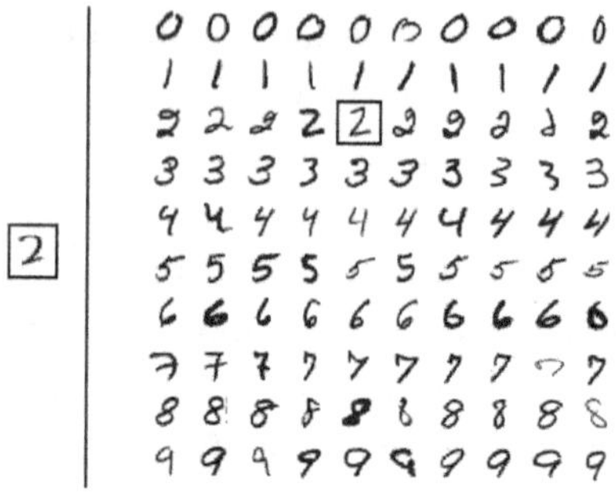

Figure 4.7 On the left: the image of a number to be classified. On the right: boxed is the nearest neighbor according to the number of matching pixels.[50]

algorithms, change their behavior as they see more *training data*. The more data they are trained on, the better they perform. Machine learning turns out to be a much more effective approach to artificial intelligence – instead of programming explicit rules, the system learns how to behave over time. Many tasks, such as facial recognition, that are now routine for machine learning systems seem completely out of reach for rule-based approaches.

The idea of teaching a machine to learn might make sense in theory, but how does one actually create such an algorithm? The following algorithm illustrates the idea. If one wants to differentiate images of handwritten digits (1, 2, 3, ...) using machine learning, one simple idea is to keep a database of all the digits that are in the training data, together with the correct *labels*, or classifications, of the images. Upon seeing a new digit, the algorithm finds the closest image in the dataset (according to some notion of distance, for example, on how many pixels the images agree), and it predicts the new digit to have the same label as its "nearest neighbor." This is illustrated in Figure 4.7. The larger the training dataset, the better the intelligent system performs. Of course, the nearest-neighbor approach is rather unsophisticated and does not come close to being able to produce the impressive results of recent systems, but it does provide some hint at what machine learning entails.

The Deep Learning Revolution

Beginning in the 2010s, artificial intelligence researchers began making remarkable progress using a machine learning technique known as *neural networks*. These advances have accelerated in recent years, leading to systems that can recognize images and speech, translate languages, generate text, and assist with complex decision-making tasks. As a result, neural-network-based methods are now rapidly transforming fields ranging from medicine and finance to transportation, science, and creative work.

The idea for neural networks began in 1943, when two Americans - a neurophysiologist, Warren McCulloch, and a logician, Walter Pitts - collaborated on a paper showing that the activity of neurons could be idealized mathematically and organized into networks that carry out logical operations.[52] In their framework, neural activity could be treated as a formal system governed by rules, making it possible to analyze aspects of reasoning using the language of logic and computation.

Then in 1958, building on these ideas, American psychologist Frank Rosenblatt introduced a learning algorithm that could automatically adjust the weights, or strengths, of connections between artificial neurons based on training examples; drawing on the notion of perception, he called it the *perceptron*.[53] Rosenblatt wrote at the time, "we are about to witness the birth of ... a machine capable of perceiving, recognizing and identifying its surroundings without any human training or control."[54] Figure 4.8 shows both a biological neuron and an artificial neuron.

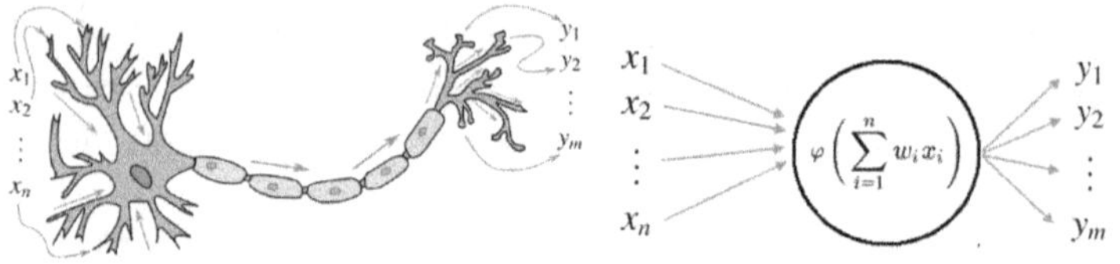

(a) A diagram of a biological neuron, with dendrites on the left, myelin sheaths in the middle, and axon terminals on the right. Signals go in the direction of the arrows.[51]

(b) A diagram of an artificial neuron. The learned weights, w_i s, multiplied by the signals x_i s are summed and then fed to a function φ, which produces the outputs, y_i s.

Figure 4.8 (a) A biological neuron; (b) an artificial neuron.

The optimism generated by early work on perceptrons persisted for roughly a decade. Then in 1969 MIT professors Marvin Minsky and Seymour Papert published a book in which they showed the limitations of perceptrons, including that they could not learn whether two arbitrary cells in an image are connected via a path of the same-colored pixels.[55] These mathematical limitations, combined with a lack of the promised empirical success, dampened the enthusiasm around neural networks. Research nevertheless continued, and by the 1980s a training algorithm called backpropagation became widely used. It provided a systematic method for training multi-layered neural networks (illustrated in Figure 4.9), which overcame many of the limitations that Minsky and Papert had identified with single-layer perceptrons.[56]

This led to a brief revival of interest in neural networks during the 1980s. By the 1990s, most of the theoretical elements for later successes were already in place, but computers were at that time not yet powerful enough to take advantage of these methods. Neural networks also lacked large datasets for training and suffered from various technical problems. As a result, other algorithms (boosting, random forests, support vector machines) became state-of-the-art, and neural networks were again dismissed by

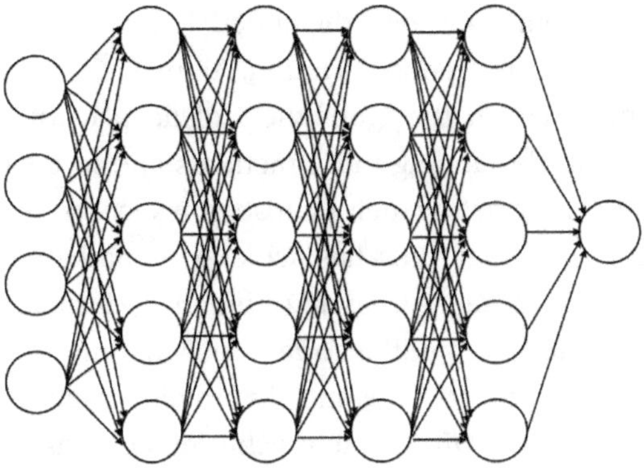

Figure 4.9 A multi-layered neural network composed of artificial neurons.

much of the AI community as promising methods that had ultimately failed.

The field was largely stagnant until around 2010, by which point the needed technology was available. Graphics processing units (GPUs), originally designed for video games, proved remarkably well-suited for the parallel computations required to train neural networks. The internet made possible the creation of massive datasets, for example one called ImageNet that has millions of labeled images. New training methods, computational models for neuron activations, and specialized neural network architectures* such as convolutional neural networks (CNNs), which are particularly effective for analyzing visual data, were also invented in the meantime. The breakthrough came in 2012 with `AlexNet`, a deep convolutional neural network that vastly outperformed all other methods in an image recognition competition and started what is now known as the *deep learning* revolution. The term deep learning refers to the large number of layers in the neural networks,

* An architecture specifies how the neurons are connected to each other, and it is usually fixed throughout the training of the neural network.

which allows them to discover the underlying structure of the data. Key figures such as Geoffrey Hinton, Yann LeCun, and Yoshua Bengio – often called the "godfathers of deep learning" – were instrumental in developing these methods and in advocating for their potential long before their mainstream success.

Since 2012, deep learning has achieved remarkable successes. Neural networks began surpassing human performance in tasks ranging from image recognition to game playing, and enabled major advances in scientific domains such as protein structure prediction and drug discovery. One notable achievement was DeepMind's `AlphaFold` system, which used neural networks to accurately predict the three-dimensional structure of proteins directly from their amino acid sequences, a longstanding problem in biology (Chapter 6 has more details on protein folding). Related approaches have since been applied to identifying candidate drug molecules and modeling molecular interactions.

Then, in 2017, a neural network architecture called the *transformer*, designed to model relationships within sequences of data, was introduced and proved especially effective for understanding and generating human language. This led to the development of large language models (LLMs) – neural networks that are trained to predict the next word in a sequence by learning from vast collections of text, a process that does not require manual labeling and can therefore scale to nearly all available written language.

Chatbots such as `ChatGPT`, which are built on top of these LLMs, are now widely used by the public to engage in informative conversations, write and debug code, draft emails and documents, summarize and reorganize notes, generate recipes, and assist with a wide range of everyday tasks. Modern LLMs contain billions of artificial neurons and represent some of the most complex computational systems ever created, enabling machines to interact with human language and reasoning at an unprecedented scale. Recent though these systems are, they are already reshaping how people think, work, and communicate.

Further Explorations

Historical Notes

In 1837, Charles Babbage designed the first general-purpose computer, which he called the "analytical engine," though he never managed to build the device. It was not until 1945 that the first general-purpose electronic computer, the ENIAC, was built following John Mauchly and J. Presper Eckert's designs. It realized Turing's idea of a universal machine. Current computers are built using architectures based on designs developed by the great mathematician John von Neumann, also in 1945. These were predated by special-purpose computers, such as Turing's 1939 Bombe, which helped crack the German Enigma codes.

Despite unjust mistreatment during his lifetime by the British government for his homosexuality, Turing is now greatly admired as the founding father of computer science, credited with establishing the field's intellectual underpinnings. Turing is also recognized as the leader of the group that broke the Enigma cipher during World War II. The Turing Award, computer science's equivalent of the Nobel Prize, is named after him. Many of the people described in this chapter indeed won this award for their stunning intellectual contributions.

- Juris Hartmanis and Richard Stearns shared the Turing Award for their paper that established the foundations of computational complexity theory.
- Stephen Cook won the Turing Award for his theories that led to the `P` vs. `NP` problem. (Leonid Levin was passed up, possibly because his discovery, though independent, came about two years later.)

- Richard Karp won the Turing Award in part for demonstrating the ubiquity of NP-complete problems.
- Michael Rabin won the Turing Award for his contributions to theoretical computer science.
- Whitfield Diffie and Martin Hellman jointly won the Turing Award for their key-exchange protocol.
- Yoshua Bengio, Geoffrey Hinton, and Yann LeCun received the Turing Award for their contributions to deep learning.*

The results of these scientists are only a sampling of the intellectual wonders that computer science has to offer.

For the Mathematically Inclined

The Diffie–Hellman key exchange protocol (illustrated with a paint analogy in Figure 4.6) is described concretely in Algorithm 4.10

1: Alice and Bob agree on a large prime number p and a base g.
2: Alice chooses a, computes $A = g^a \bmod p$, and sends A to Bob.
3: Bob chooses b and computes $B = g^b \bmod p$, and sends B to Alice.
4: Alice computes the shared secret $S_A = B^a \bmod p$.
5: Bob computes the shared secret $S_B = A^b \bmod p$.
6: The shared secret S is S_A for Alice and S_B for Bob, where $S_A = S_B$.

Algorithm 4.10: The Diffie–Hellman key exchange protocol.

Here is the correspondence to the paint analogy. The common paint is determined by p and g. Alice's secret paint is a, and Bob's secret paint is b. The mix that Alice sends to Bob is $A = g^a \bmod p$,

* Geoffrey Hinton and John Hopfield also won the Nobel Prize in physics for their contributions to neural networks.

and the mix that Bob sends to Alice is $B = g^b \bmod p$. The full mix is $B^a \bmod p = A^b \bmod p$. It is not hard to see that they both have the same secret in the end:

$$A^b \bmod p = g^{ab} \bmod p = g^{ba} \bmod p = B^a \bmod p.$$

Eve observes p, g, A, and B. But since she does not know a or b, to compute S, Eve needs to determine which a gives $A = g^a \bmod p$ or which b gives $B = g^b \bmod p$ from the other values. This is called the *discrete logarithm* problem because it requires finding a logarithm in the context of a discrete object called a finite group. The discrete logarithm problem is believed to be hard (i.e., thought not to be in P), and if this assumption is correct, Eve cannot discover the shared secret under reasonable computation constraints when a, b, and p are sufficiently large (g can be a small number).

The quantities have the following names in public-key cryptography: a and b are Alice's and Bob's secret keys, respectively; A and B are Alice's and Bob's public keys, respectively; S is the shared secret key. The function $f_{p,g}(a) = g^a \bmod p$ is a candidate one-way function since it is easy to compute but believed hard to invert. The discrete logarithm problem and other candidate one-way functions lie at the foundations of cryptography.

Additional Reading

Douglas Hofstadter's celebrated book, *Gödel, Escher, Bach: an Eternal Golden Braid,* gives an elegant introduction to connections among mathematics, computation, and intelligence. *The New Turing Omnibus* by Alexander K. Dewdney contains a broad and accessible collection of articles on a variety of topics in computing.

5

Reality in Superposition
Quantum Mechanics

Quantum mechanics can trace its origins to a seventeenth-century debate between two giants of science, Isaac Newton and Christiaan Huygens, about the nature of light. Newton had some compelling evidence that light was composed of particles – he argued that the sharpness of shadows, as well as experiments showing that a prism splits light into constituent colors, pointed toward the particle explanation. Huygens, conversely, had convincing arguments that light must be a wave – his wave theory was much more easily able to explain various phenomena involving refraction and diffraction. This Newton–Huygens debate took around 200 years to resolve and even longer to be fully understood, with the advent of quantum mechanics. This core mystery surrounding the "dual nature" of light, as well as other phenomena, is explained in this chapter.

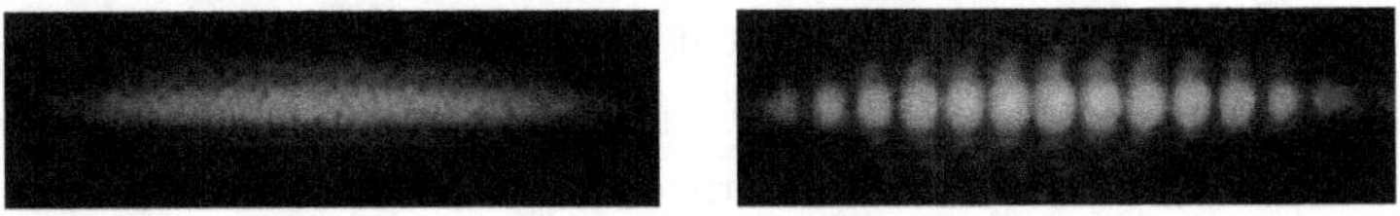

(a) Typical results from a single-slit setup.

(b) Typical results from a double-slit setup.

Figure 5.1 Brighter regions correspond to areas on the screen hit by more light.[59]

In physics, quantum theory best explains the behavior of the very small, for example, of particles like electrons. Even people who know nothing else about quantum mechanics have probably heard that it is very strange. Danish physicist Niels Bohr, who developed the model of the atom and helped found quantum mechanics, famously said that "those who are not shocked when they first come across quantum theory cannot possibly have understood it."[57]

Young's Double-slit Experiment

The now-famous *double-slit experiment* was first performed by the British polymath Thomas Young at the beginning of the nineteenth century.[58] After verifying the known phenomenon that light sent through a single slit peaks in brightness at the center of the screen and fades toward the edges, Young opened up a second slit nearby and again projected a beam of light. He observed that the opening of a second slit produced an *interference pattern* on the screen. While giving light more avenues to travel made the screen brighter in some places, as expected, the light also became *less intense* in others, in an alternating pattern as illustrated in Figure 5.1.

At the time, Young's double-slit experiment still admitted what physicists would later call a *classical* explanation – that is, an explanation in which light was assumed to follow definite, well-defined behavior at all times, without invoking any fundamentally new rules of nature like quantum theory. Just as two waves crossing at sea can produce a beautiful pattern of amplifications and cancellations, light seemed to behave similarly: The apparent light waves going through the two slits amplified each other in some places and canceled out in others. The main remaining question appeared to be about what medium light waves propagate through. Just as ocean waves propagate through water and sound waves through the air, so too light waves were conjectured to propagate through something, which was beautifully named the "luminiferous aether" (now called "ether").

The double-slit experiment's truly mysterious nature, therefore, did not become apparent for some time. Over a hundred years later, in the early twentieth century, scientists, including giants like Max Planck and Albert Einstein, began producing compelling explanations for a variety of phenomena that required viewing light as consisting of individual particles called *photons*. Then, finally, in the early 1920s, American physicist Arthur Compton demonstrated to the satisfaction of most skeptics that light cannot simply be a wave by experimentally showing that individual photons can interact with charged particles.[60] This effect took the eponymous name "Compton scattering."

So, is light a particle or a wave after all? A common misconception often taught to schoolchildren and repeated in popular science books is that light is "both." Taken literally, however, this phrasing is misleading and tends to obscure rather than clarify what quantum mechanics actually says. Light indeed arrives in discrete units called photons. The genuinely surprising quantum insight, first proposed by the French physicist Louis de Broglie and later confirmed experimentally, is that photons – and in fact all physical objects, including electrons, atoms, and even molecules – are subject to quantum effects that make them *behave* as waves.[61] This idea is known as *wave–particle duality*.

One way to demonstrate this conclusively is to repeat Young's double-slit experiment using more precise instruments to send one photon at a time instead of a beam of light. When this experiment is performed using modern technology, the light particles collect on the screen in the same interference pattern. It means that the passing of a single photon through one slit interferes *with itself* passing through the other slit! The same experiment, producing the same interference pattern, can be repeated with electrons and, as of 2019, even with large molecules consisting of thousands of atoms.[62] These results cannot be explained by classical physics, where particles might pass through one slit or the other, perhaps randomly. Instead, the particles in the double-slit experiment enter a mysterious state that physicists call a quantum *superposition* of the two trajectories.*

It is important to note that if the experimental setup allows the two alternatives to be distinguished through interaction with a detector or the environment (as occurs in a measurement), then the interference pattern disappears due to *decoherence*, the process by which interference effects are effectively suppressed by interactions with the environment, and predictions from classical physics apply. Because macroscopic objects are very hard to isolate, it also explains why, even though all objects are subject to quantum effects, people do not have personal experience with quantum mechanics.† This phenomenon has also prompted philosophical discussion about the meaning of measurement in quantum mechanics and the transition from quantum to classical behavior.[63]

* It is also wrong to say that a particle in a superposition of two trajectories takes "both" trajectories. Part of the challenge of understanding quantum mechanics is that superposition defies intuition.

† One of the difficulties of building a quantum computer is maintaining the coherence of its system, as described later in this chapter. If and when such computers come into everyday use, then people will begin to see quantum effects in their lives in the form of faster calculations for certain problems.

American physicist Richard Feynman – who, in addition to extending quantum theory to electromagnetism, was also an accomplished expositor of physics – wrote that the double-slit experiment in itself "contain[s] all of the mystery of quantum mechanics."[64] While the double-slit experiment vividly illustrates this "quantum weirdness," Feynman also described an arguably stranger setup that brings these ideas into even sharper focus, revealing aspects of quantum behavior that defy classical intuition.[65] This thought experiment was later presented in an especially clear form by the philosopher David Albert, who brought it to a wider audience.[66] This setup will be referred to in this chapter as the "strange experiment." The following sections introduce the devices involved, which are interesting in their own right, before turning to the experiment that makes their combined effect especially striking.

A Dual-path Interferometer

An *interferometer*, as its name suggests, is used to measure interference of the sort produced in the double-slit experiment. Interferometers come in different configurations, but they generally work by merging beams of particles to produce patterns of interference to be analyzed. They are important tools in both science and industry and are also useful for probing the laws of physics. A famous recent example is the Laser Interferometer Gravitational-Wave Observatory (LIGO), which in 2016 announced the first experimental observation of gravitational waves produced by a collision of two black holes, confirming a century-old theoretical prediction of Einstein's general theory of relativity (Chapter 3 discussed this theory) and inaugurating the field of gravitational-wave astronomy.[67]

The history of interferometry has involved numerous technical advances by many scientists and engineers. French mathematician

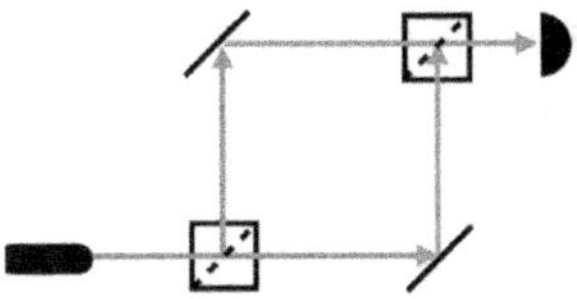

Figure 5.2 A Mach–Zehnder interferometer. The solid diagonal lines are mirrors, the boxes are beam splitters/recombiners, a particle source is on the bottom left, and the solid semicircle is a detector. The particles follow the gray arrow directions.

and scientist François Arago is credited with building the very first interferometer in the early 1800s to measure the refractive index of air, a physical property that determines how light propagates in this medium. He used a design in which multiple beams travel along the same path throughout the experiment. After over 50 years of improvements in interferometry, American physicist Albert Michelson created a more flexible *dual-path* construction, in which the beams travel along two distinct paths.

Proposed by the Swiss physicist Ludwig Zehnder in 1891 and refined by the Austrian physicist and chemist Ludwig Mach the following year, the Mach–Zehnder configuration is a more versatile improvement of the Michelson interferometer.[68,69] Its basic design is illustrated in Figure 5.2. A Mach–Zehnder interferometer uses a splitter to divide a beam of particles into two paths and another one to recombine the paths. A detector then records the resulting interference pattern,* though for the purpose of illustrating Feynman's strange experiment, all that will be required is to examine the number of particles hitting each detector. The Mach–Zehnder interferometer will comprise the framework for the experiment. The

* If a beam is split and recombined with no relative phase difference between the two paths, nothing visibly interesting happens. An interference pattern appears only when a phase difference is introduced, for example by changing one path length or passing one beam through a different medium.

main component is a device that can split electrons according to their spin along a given axis.

Spin Selectors

In 1922, the German physicists Otto Stern and Walther Gerlach designed an apparatus to confirm the theory that electron *spin* – a nonclassical form of angular momentum – when measured along any direction will always take only one of two particular values.[70] Despite the name, spin is not literal rotation. Instead, it is an intrinsic property of particles that obeys the same mathematical rules as angular momentum but has no classical analogue. The two possible values for spin are called spin *up* and spin *down*. Given a *vector* $\vec{z}$ specifying a direction in space, the electrons with spin up when measured along $\vec{z}$ are called z_+, and those with spin down are called z_-.*

The Stern–Gerlach device uses a magnetic field that is stronger in some regions than in others to split a beam of electrons† along $\vec{z}$ into two distinct beams, one consisting of z_+ and the other of z_-. Electrons from a "spin-unpolarized" source, such as a hot filament, will come out in equal proportion between z_+ and z_- along any choice of direction $\vec{z}$. Figure 5.3a illustrates the Stern–Gerlach splitter.

Physicists can run experiments chaining multiple Stern–Gerlach devices to check, for example, whether the spin along a direction changes after measurement. As expected, it does not. As illustrated in Figure 5.3b, filtering out all of the z_- electrons and then checking the spin again will show a stream with only z_+ electrons remaining.

* Outside quantum mechanics, the axes $\vec{x}$, $\vec{y}$, and $\vec{z}$ are often used in that order. In quantum mechanics, the convention is to make $\vec{z}$ the primary axis, followed by $\vec{x}$, then $\vec{y}$.

† Stern and Gerlach originally used silver atoms, but their device can be adapted for electrons using more sophisticated techniques to compensate for their negative charge.

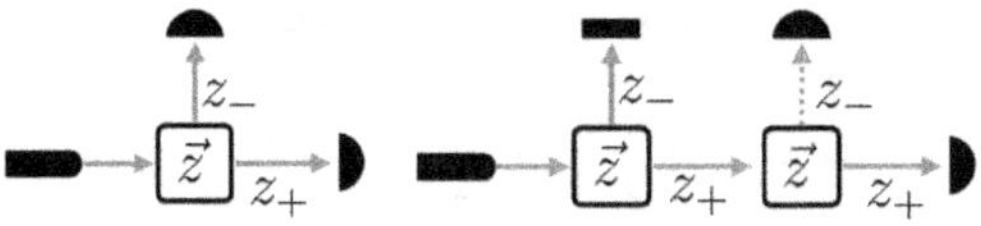

(a) The basic Stern–Gerlach setup.

(b) Two Stern–Gerlach devices in a row.

Figure 5.3 (a) A source of unpolarized electrons is on the left, the spin splitter along the given axis is shown in the middle, and the semicircles are detectors. (b) The first device is connected to a second one after the z_- electrons are filtered out. No z_- electrons hit the top detector. No electrons end up taking the dotted path.

A slightly more complicated experiment, however, elucidates another strange aspect of quantum mechanics involving Heisenberg's *uncertainty principle*. The uncertainty principle was originally the result of a thought experiment about the impossibility of simultaneously knowing a particle's position and momentum arbitrarily well. The German physicist Werner Heisenberg argued that a short-wavelength (therefore high-energy) photon needs to be used to measure a particle's position accurately, but the high energy would impart momentum to the particle, changing it. Conversely, low-energy (therefore long-wavelength) photons could measure a particle's momentum without much disturbing it, but their long wavelength would give little information about the particle's position. And no matter the wavelength used, there will be a tradeoff.[71]

The uncertainty principle extends beyond position and momentum to many other pairs of physical quantities, including electron spin measured along different directions. For spin, the relevant feature is that measurements along perpendicular axes are incompatible: Determining the spin along one direction necessarily disrupts information about the spin along a perpendicular direction. As a result, if electrons with spin z_- are first filtered out so that only z_+

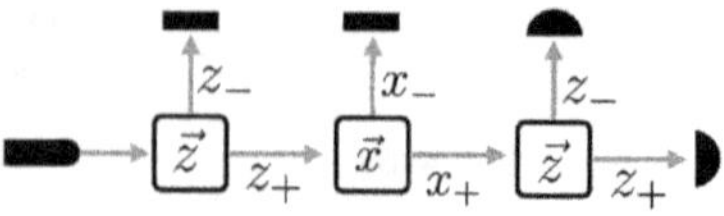

Figure 5.4 A third Stern–Gerlach device is chained in a row. The first device filters by spin along $\vec{z}$, the middle one filters according to spin along the perpendicular direction $\vec{x}$, and the third device once again measures spin along $\vec{z}$. Electrons with both z_+ and z_- spins are now detected in the final measurement.

electrons remain, and those electrons are then filtered according to their spin along the perpendicular direction $\vec{x}$, the act of measuring the $\vec{x}$ spin erases the prior information about the $\vec{z}$ spin. When the spin along $\vec{z}$ is measured again, the electrons are found equally likely to be z_+ or z_-. If this were not the case, it would be possible to prepare electrons with well-defined spin components along both $\vec{z}$ and $\vec{x}$ simultaneously, contradicting the uncertainty principle. This behavior is illustrated in Figure 5.4.

The Strange Experiment

The last step is to combine the Stern–Gerlach and Mach–Zehnder experiments. The first step is to replace the beam splitter in the Mach–Zehnder interferometer with a Stern–Gerlach device that splits electrons according to their spin along a vector $\vec{x}$. For the beam recombiner, a uniform magnetic field can be used to combine the "spin-polarized" x_+ and x_- beams without affecting their spins. Such a device is sometimes referred to as a "spin interferometer."

The second step is to use another Stern–Gerlach device to first filter out the spin-down electrons along a direction $\vec{z}$ perpendicular to $\vec{x}$. Finally, a third Stern–Gerlach device is added to again test the

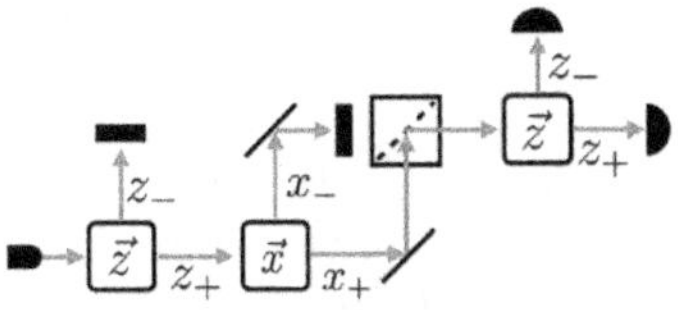

(a) The top-left path is blocked.

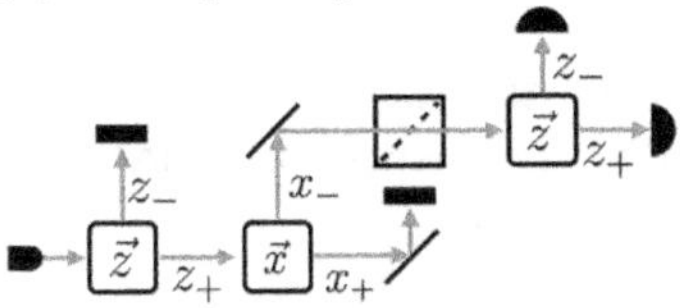

(b) The bottom-right path is blocked.

Figure 5.5 A combined Stern–Gerlach/Mach–Zehnder setup with a blocked path. As in Figure 5.4, the spins along $\vec{z}$ become up and down with equal probability at the end.

spin along $\vec{z}$ after the recombination of the beams in the Mach–Zehnder interferometer.

Before proceeding to analyze what happens here, an observation should be made. If the top-left path is blocked, as illustrated in Figure 5.5a, then the same experiment as in Figure 5.4 results, with the same outcome - namely, the final detectors record that the electrons are z_+ and z_- with equal probability. Similarly, if the bottom-right path is blocked, as illustrated in Figure 5.5b, then it is the x_+ electrons that are filtered out, but again the result is the same, because the uncertainty principle forbids preserving definite spin information along two perpendicular directions.

So, what should happen if neither path is blocked? Classical intuition indicates that the result should again be a mix of z_+ and z_- electrons. After all, when either path was blocked, the detector registered both z_+ and z_- electrons, so one would expect that opening both paths would simply produce the combined result of the two individual paths. But that is not what happens: instead, the final detector picks up no z_- electrons! This striking result,

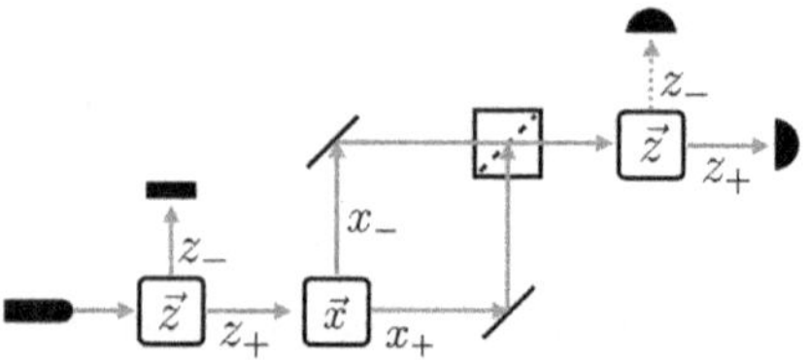

Figure 5.6 A combined Stern–Gerlach/Mach–Zehnder setup with no blocked path. As in the experiment depicted in Figure 5.3b, no z_- electrons take the dotted path.

illustrated in Figure 5.6, defies classical probability and highlights the counterintuitive nature of quantum superposition.

The keen reader might ask: Wasn't the spin along $\vec{x}$ measured? Did this chapter not just explain that this makes the spin along $\vec{z}$ uncertain again? The answer is that, no, the spin along $\vec{x}$ was never measured. Just like the double-slit interference pattern is created only when the experimenter does not measure which slit the particles traveled through, here the two alternatives interfere with each other because the electron remains in a superposition rather than settling into a definite $\vec{x}$ spin state. The recombination of the beams erases any information about which path was taken. That is why the spin along $\vec{z}$ can be determined. Of course, if the experimenter actually measures which paths are taken by the electrons – by allowing the environment or a device to permanently distinguish between them – then this effect goes away, and the $\vec{z}$ spin becomes "reset" again.

To account for results such as double-slit interference and the strange experiment, Max Born, Erwin Schrödinger, and others had to reinvent how probability is viewed to agree with the new surprising experiments. They introduced the idea of *amplitudes*, which (to oversimplify) allow probabilistic calculations to be performed with negative numbers that can cancel each other out. Quantum mechanics can thereby produce elegant and unifying formulas that predict these and many other phenomena, but the meaning of these equations continues to cause debate.

Quantum Computing

Despite debates surrounding the interpretation of its equations, quantum mechanics works wonderfully as a theory for understanding many phenomena, and its predictions have been confirmed to extraordinary precision across a vast range of experiments. For example, quantum mechanics explains why atoms are stable: Classical mechanics wrongly predicts that electrons in the atom should collapse into the nucleus due to its attractive force, but the Heisenberg uncertainty principle explains that as an electron gets confined closer to the nucleus, the precision in its position would make its momentum become too uncertain and give it enough motion to resist the pull of the electric force from the nucleus.

Advances in quantum mechanics have also led to incredibly useful technologies: light-emitting diode (LED) lights that illuminate homes, magnetic resonance imaging (MRI) scanners that reveal the body's inner workings, and even some touchscreens.* While exploring these applications in detail lies beyond the scope of this book, it may be insightful to focus on one particular developing technology: quantum computers. These machines not only represent an exciting possibility at the forefront of science, but they also connect nicely to the strange experiment.

A quantum computer uses *qubits* (quantum bits), which can be put into superposition. Unlike a classical bit, which must be either

* Another counterintuitive quantum mechanical phenomenon called tunneling says that particles, due to their wave nature, have a nonzero probability of appearing in places that classical mechanics says they shouldn't be. Some specialized touchscreens make use of tunneling by detecting electrons that cross a barrier when the screen is pressed.

0 or 1, a qubit can be prepared in a state where neither value is definite until a measurement is made. When multiple qubits are present, quantum mechanics also allows a distinct phenomenon called *entanglement*, in which the qubits are described by a single joint quantum state that cannot be reduced to independent states of the individual qubits.* It is this shared structure of the state that quantum computers exploit, allowing information to be processed in ways that have no classical analogue.

To build intuition for superposition in a single qubit, it is helpful to use a visual analogy such as the Mach–Zehnder interferometer illustrated in Figure 5.2. One path can represent the value 0, and the other path can represent the value 1. Running particles through the machine prepares a superposed state in which both possibilities contribute, not as separate outcomes but as parts of a single quantum state. Different quantum operations can then be applied to these alternatives so that, when they are carefully recombined and measured, interference effects produce a result that would be impossible without superposition.

In 1985 physicist David Deutsch was the first to theoretically demonstrate that quantum computers could gain an advantage over classical ones.[72] He imagined a "black box" f that takes a binary (0 or 1) input and also has a binary output. As shown in Table 5.7, such an f must either be "constant" ($f(0) = f(1)$) or "balanced" ($f(0) \neq f(1)$). The goal in his problem is to determine which type (constant or balanced) this black box is.

A classical computer clearly needs to probe the box twice – first putting a 0 and then a 1 and comparing the resulting outputs. But it turns out that a quantum computer can do it in just one probe.

* Entanglement is not limited to qubits: Collections of quantum objects can, in principle, become entangled. In an entangled state, measuring one object can reveal information about the others, even when they are far apart. However, this does not allow faster-than-light communication, despite frequent portrayals to the contrary in science fiction.

Table 5.7 All possible black box functions with an input of 0 or 1 and an output of 0 or 1. There are only four such functions: Two are constant and two are balanced.

Black box	$f(0)$	$f(1)$	**Type**
1	0	0	constant
2	1	1	constant
3	0	1	balanced
4	1	0	balanced

The general idea is to apply a transformation to one part of the qubit's superposed state but not the other; in the interferometer picture, this means acting on one path while the particle is still inside the device. If the function is balanced, the two contributions cancel when the paths are recombined, whereas no such cancellation occurs if the black box is constant. The resulting measurement can be arranged to give 1 if the function is balanced and 0 if it is constant.

In certain cases, quantum computers can theoretically give speedups of this kind. These advantages arise for problems with a structure that allows many alternatives to be explored coherently and then made to interfere, so that incorrect possibilities cancel while correct ones reinforce; well-known examples include integer factoring, the discrete logarithm problem,* and the simulation of quantum systems themselves. For other problems, the advantage is not so clear. It is a popular misconception that a quantum computer can always have an "exponential speedup" over a classical one by trying all possibilities at once (2 possibilities for 1 qubit, 4 for 2, 8 for

* The "For the Mathematically Inclined" section of Chapter 4 discusses the discrete logarithm problem. Many widely used cryptographic protocols rely on the presumed difficulty of these problems and would need to be redesigned if large-scale quantum computers become practical.

3, and so on, with 2^n possibilities for n), but that is not accurate. The quantum advantage needs to be carefully leveraged via properly designed "cancellations," like in testing for whether a function is constant or balanced, or the result will be lost in the measurement.

Most computer scientists and physicists think that it should be possible to build working quantum computers, but many practical engineering challenges remain. The biggest challenge is decoherence – when qubits interact with their classical environments, they lose their quantum states, because even extremely small, unintended interactions can disrupt the superpositions on which quantum computation relies. Another major issue is errors: Quantum operations must be carried out with great precision, and small imperfections in timing, control, or isolation can accumulate in ways that are far more damaging than in classical systems. These error rates need to be reduced before modern error-correction techniques can make the entire system operate reliably.

If and when working quantum computers are finally created, they may not transform everyday society, but they will represent a monumental achievement of human understanding, ingenuity, and innovation.

Further Explorations

Historical Notes

Young's double-slit experiment and subsequent work by others in the early 1800s solidified empirical support for the wave theory of light, which before that was only supported by theoretical principles from Christiaan Huygens, Augustin-Jean Fresnel, and others. From then until the 1900s, most of the progress, or its lack, consisted mostly of scientists searching for hints of the conjectured luminiferous ether and failing to detect it. The most famous of these experiments was performed by Michelson and Morley in 1887. It is described in more detail in Chapter 3.

In 1900 Max Planck gave some of the first theoretical backing for the particle theory of light, indirectly challenging the wave theory. Then, in 1905, Albert Einstein's discovery of the photoelectric effect gave more strong theoretical evidence for the particle nature of light. That same "miraculous year," Einstein produced his famous special theory of relativity, which eliminated the need for the ether to explain electromagnetic phenomena.

The history of quantum mechanics is full of many surprising insights, only a few of which were described in order to set up the strange experiment. Although the Nobel Prize is by no means a perfect measure of scientific insight, it is worth noting that quantum mechanics was, for a long time, a fount of Nobel Prizes. Many scientists mentioned in this chapter ended up winning the Nobel for their contributions, including

- Niels Bohr for understanding atomic structure,
- Arthur Compton for Compton scattering,
- Max Planck for discovering the quanta,
- Albert Einstein for the photoelectric effect,*
- Louis de Broglie for understanding that electrons and other objects are also subject to wave–particle duality,
- Richard Feynman for the quantum theory of electrodynamics,
- Werner Heisenberg for the uncertainty principle and other fundamental contributions to quantum mechanics,
- Otto Stern for the molecular ray method and the discovery of the magnetic moment of the proton,†
- Max Born for his statistical interpretation of the wavefunction, and
- Erwin Schrödinger for his eponymous equation that governs the quantum state of a system.

* Surprisingly, Einstein did not win the Nobel Prize for the theory of relativity. At the time, the theory of relativity was too radical for some physicists, but his stature was such that failing to award him the Nobel would hurt the prestige of the prize itself. Awarding Einstein the Nobel Prize for the photoelectric effect was the agreed-upon compromise.

† It is worth noting that Stern's Nobel was not awarded for the Stern–Gerlach device.

This list is not intended to be comprehensive. Other Nobel Prize-winning contributors to quantum mechanics - including Eugene Wigner, Enrico Fermi, Paul Dirac, and Wolfgang Pauli - do not appear here.

For the Mathematically Inclined

The mathematics here is not completely formal. Instead, it is meant to give mathematically inclined readers a very basic idea of how particles can be in superposition and how probabilities can amplify (constructive interference) or cancel each other out (destructive interference).

A *vector* is an ordered list of numbers, often used to represent the state of a system in a compact mathematical form. Let a particle having spin-up along $\vec{z}$ be represented by a pair of numbers (a two-dimensional vector) with 1 in the first coordinate and 0 in the second. And spin-down would take on values 0 and 1 for the first and second coordinates, respectively. This is to ensure these two vectors are *orthogonal,* a generalization of perpendicular. In $|\cdot\rangle$ notation for representing a quantum state ψ (known as Dirac or braket notation), this would be written as $|z_+\rangle = \binom{1}{0}$ and $|z_-\rangle = \binom{0}{1}$.

In quantum mechanics, the probability of any event coming about after measurement is equal to the square of the absolute value of its *amplitude,* so state vectors need to be *unit length,* which means the squares of the components need to add up to 1.

Recall that knowing the spin along $\vec{z}$ would make the spin along $\vec{x}$ equally likely to be up and down. So, $|x_+\rangle = \frac{1}{\sqrt{2}}\left(\binom{1}{0} + \binom{0}{1}\right) = \frac{1}{\sqrt{2}}\binom{1}{1}$. The $\frac{1}{\sqrt{2}}$ *normalizes* the vector to make it unit length.* One

* To make the length of a vector 1, it should be rescaled so that the sum of the squares of its components needs to add to 1. So, $\left(\frac{1}{\sqrt{2}}(1)\right)^2 + \left(\frac{1}{\sqrt{2}}(1)\right)^2 = \frac{1}{2} + \frac{1}{2} = 1.$

way to make $|x_+\rangle$ orthogonal to $|x_-\rangle$ is to set $|x_-\rangle = \frac{1}{\sqrt{2}}\binom{1}{-1}$. To summarize,

$$|z_+\rangle = \binom{1}{0}, \quad |z_-\rangle = \binom{0}{1}, \quad |x_+\rangle = \frac{1}{\sqrt{2}}\binom{1}{1}, \quad |x_-\rangle = \frac{1}{\sqrt{2}}\binom{1}{-1}.$$

To analyze the case of three chained Stern–Gerlach machines (Figure 5.4):

(i) Particles from the source are "spin-unpolarized," meaning that with respect to the $\vec{z}$ direction, the beam consists of electrons that are equally likely to be in the states $|z_+\rangle$ and $|z_-\rangle$. When the spin along $\vec{z}$ is measured using the first Stern–Gerlach device, an electron emerges in either the $|z_+\rangle$ or $|z_-\rangle$ state, each with probability $\frac{1}{2}$.

(ii) The electrons in state $|z_+\rangle$ now go into a Stern–Gerlach device for measuring $\vec{x}$. Conveniently, $|z_+\rangle = \frac{1}{\sqrt{2}}|x_+\rangle + \frac{1}{\sqrt{2}}|x_-\rangle$. This can be checked as follows: $\frac{1}{\sqrt{2}}\frac{1}{\sqrt{2}}\binom{1}{1} + \frac{1}{\sqrt{2}}\frac{1}{\sqrt{2}}\binom{1}{-1} = \frac{1}{2}\binom{1}{1} + \frac{1}{2}\binom{1}{-1} = \binom{1}{0} = |z_+\rangle$. So both the $|x_+\rangle$ and $|x_-\rangle$ outcomes are equally likely.

(iii) Those electrons that come out in the $|x_+\rangle$ state are sent to the third device. Similarly, in step (ii), one can check that $|x_+\rangle = \frac{1}{\sqrt{2}}|z_-\rangle + \frac{1}{\sqrt{2}}|z_+\rangle$, and by the same logic as in step (i), the final measurement along $\vec{z}$ comes out as before, with $|z_+\rangle$ and $|z_-\rangle$ equally likely.

The same calculation holds for Figure 5.5a, and a similar one holds for Figure 5.5b. But what happens in the strange experiment (Figure 5.6) itself? Part (i) obviously remains as before. Part (ii) now has the double-path device, where the electron enters superposition as $\frac{1}{\sqrt{2}}|x_+\rangle + \frac{1}{\sqrt{2}}|x_-\rangle$ and is recombined in the superposition state. Part (iii) uses the observation that $\frac{1}{\sqrt{2}}|x_+\rangle + \frac{1}{\sqrt{2}}|x_-\rangle = |z_+\rangle$ as before, so only z_+ electrons are detected. It takes some practice, but this mathematical view makes everything simpler!

Finally, it is worthwhile to note that while the above discussion purposely avoided complex numbers (which involve $i = \sqrt{-1}$), the mathematics behind quantum mechanics requires complex numbers in general. In the case of measuring spin, to "fit" a third orthogonal $\vec{y}$ axis, the definitions $|y_+\rangle = \frac{1}{\sqrt{2}}\binom{1}{i}$ and $|y_-\rangle = \frac{1}{\sqrt{2}}\binom{1}{-i}$ could be used. An amplitude can also take complex values, and since its associated probability is the *square of its absolute value,* it is never negative. For example, filtering spin-up electrons along $\vec{y}$ and then measuring their spin along $\vec{x}$ would involve looking at $|y_+\rangle = \frac{1}{2}(1+i)|x_+\rangle + \frac{1}{2}(1-i)|x_-\rangle$. The amplitudes of both $|x_+\rangle$ and $|x_-\rangle$ are the complex numbers $\frac{1}{2} + \frac{i}{2}$ and $\frac{1}{2} - \frac{i}{2}$, respectively.

Additional Reading

A classical and engaging exploration of quantum mechanics can be found in the book *In Search of Schrödinger's Cat: Quantum Physics and Reality* by astrophysicist John Gribbin. For a more mathematically sophisticated treatment, focused on philosophical insights, the book *Quantum Mechanics and Experience*[66] by David Z. Albert stands out – the strange experiment at the heart of this chapter appears prominently in his book.

6

The Code Within
Molecular Genetics

When, in 1865, the Augustinian friar and abbot Gregor Mendel famously crossed purple-flowered peas with white-flowered ones, he did not see light purple flowers. Instead, the next generation was entirely purple-flowered. The following generation, however, had a mix of purple and white-flowered plants in approximately a 3:1 ratio, as illustrated in Figure 6.1.[73] These results contradicted the then-prevailing theory of inheritance called "blending," which proposed that offspring would inherit a mixture of their parents' traits.

Surprising as Mendel's work was, it caused little stir in the scientific community. Yet it should have sparked a scientific revolution, for it presaged that underlying the blueprint to life was a discrete, and not a continuous, mechanism. Only a discrete, or digital, system of inheritance – one in which information is stored in separable, well-defined units rather than as a smoothly varying

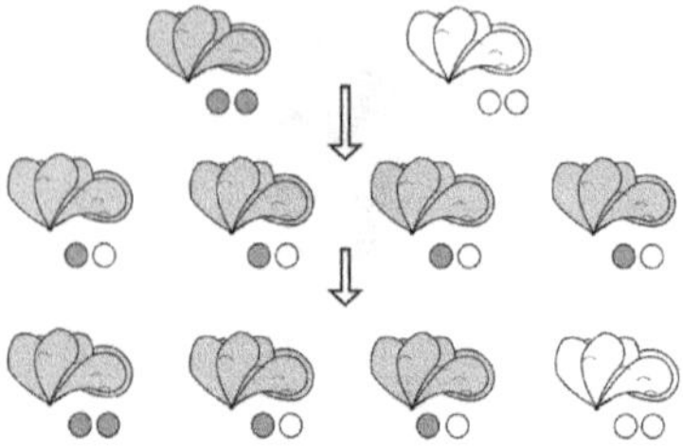

Figure 6.1 In the first generation (top row), a pure-bred purple-flowered plant (●●) is crossed with a pure-bred white-flowered plant (○○), producing offspring that are all purple. The second generation (second row) consists of these offspring, each of which carries one purple and one white version of the same flower-color gene. These different versions of a single gene are called alleles and are denoted here by ● for purple and ○ for white. When plants from the second generation (●○) are intercrossed to produce the third generation (bottom row), each parent randomly contributes either a ● or a ○ allele to each offspring. This yields a genetic ratio of 1/4 (●●), 1/2 (●○), and 1/4 (○○) (a 1:2:1 ratio), which appears as an approximately 3:1 ratio of purple to white flowers, since the ● allele is dominant over ○.

quantity – could explain how traits could be passed across generations without blending, particularly in the clear mathematical ratios that Mendel observed. Instead, it took until the twentieth century for the significance of his result to become recognized and a half century more until this scientific journey culminated in uncovering the physical form of the genetic code itself.

The importance of a discrete system of storing genes cannot be overstated, as discrete systems allow for error correction, replication, and long-term stability, among other desirable properties that are nearly impossible to maintain in analog (nondigital) forms of information storage. Without a discrete storage mechanism, it is hard to imagine how life could have evolved. For this reason, the former president of the Sloan Kettering Institute and American physician Lewis Thomas proclaimed that "the greatest single achievement of nature to date was surely the invention of the DNA molecule."[74]

The Structure of DNA

In 1900, Carl Correns, Hugo de Vries, and Erich von Tschermak, all botanists, independently rediscovered Mendel's seminal work. Later that same year, English biologist William Bateson translated Mendel's original paper into English and promoted it in scientific circles. By that point, its significance could be better understood, and scientists became interested in understanding the hidden discrete mechanism underlying inheritance. It was also around that time that the term *gene* came into use to describe Mendelian units of heredity and *genetics* to describe the study of genes.

The first major advances in determining where genes are stored were made a few years later by American biologist Walter Sutton, who experimented on grasshoppers, and by German biologist Theodor Boveri, who experimented on sea urchins. They independently gathered convincing evidence that hereditary information was contained in thread-like structures in cells called chromosomes (whose structure was eventually understood as depicted in Figure 6.2). They correctly hypothesized, in what became known as the Boveri–Sutton theory, that chromosomes form the entire basis for Mendelian heredity.[75] Subsequent work by American biologist Thomas Hunt Morgan further confirmed and expanded upon these findings, establishing the chromosomal theory of inheritance.[76]

By that point in the early 1900s, scientists already knew that chromosomes are primarily composed of deoxyribonucleic acid (DNA) and proteins, but which of these stored the genes was debated. It was known that DNA consists of units called nucleotides that are differentiated by four different nitrogen bases: adenine (`A`), cytosine (`C`), guanine (`G`), and thymine (`T`). Just four different DNA

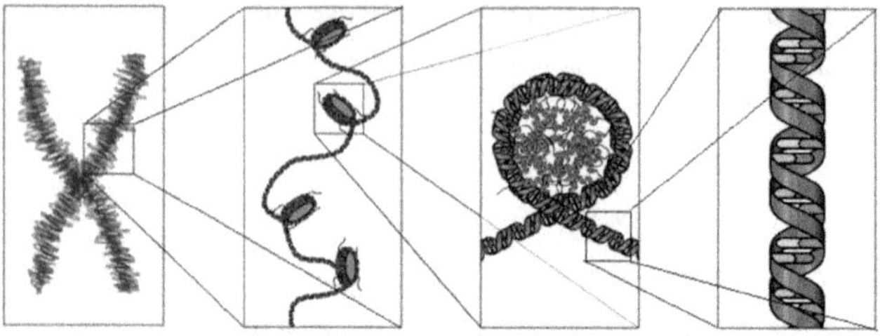

Figure 6.2 The scientific picture that eventually emerged, of chromosomes (left) being formed of DNA (right) wrapped around proteins (middle two).[77]

nucleotides were thought to be insufficiently rich to encode all of the needed genetic information,[78] so scientists believed for a time that genetic information was more likely to be stored in the much more complex proteins. This concern seems naive in hindsight – computers can store and process an immense amount of information using just two symbols (0 and 1), so four "letters" are more than sufficient.

It took researchers four more decades to determine that it was indeed the DNA that stored genetic material. In 1944, Rockefeller Institute scientists Oswald Avery, Colin MacLeod, and Maclyn McCarty conducted a clever experiment, in which they converted harmless bacteria into disease-causing bacteria by extracting DNA, but not proteins, from the latter and transferring it to the former. This indicated that the essential information was stored in DNA and not in proteins.[79] This was later conclusively proven by an even more definitive experiment in 1952 by American geneticists Alfred Hershey and Martha Chase.[80]

Determining that genes were stored in DNA was an important advance, but its molecular structure was at that point still unknown. Thus, in the early 1950s a race among several prominent research groups began to determine how this molecule actually stored and

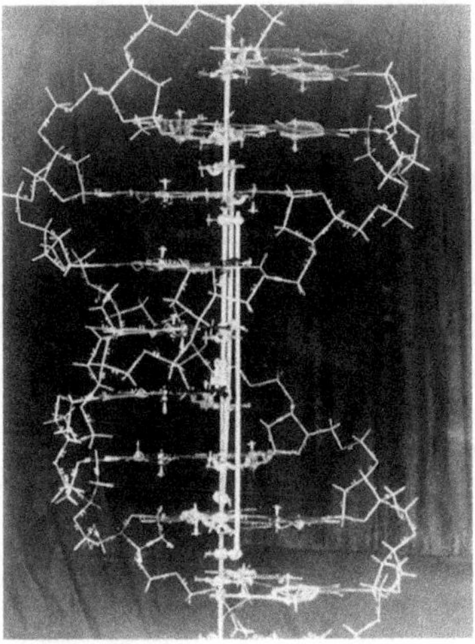

(a) The original Watson and Crick DNA model. (The central pole holding up the structure is not part of the model.)[81]

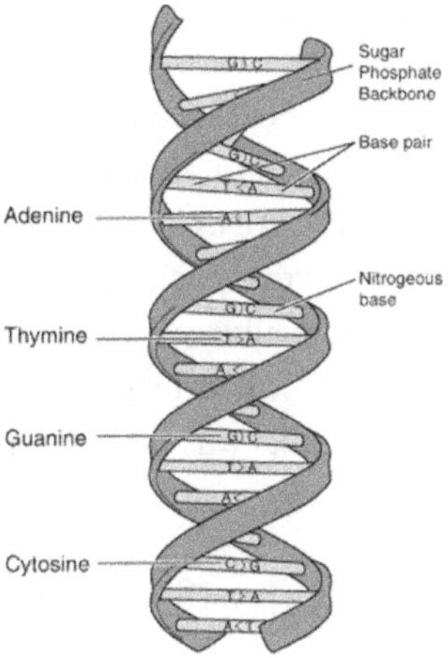

(b) A more abstract schematic of the Watson and Crick model, illustrating where the base pairs interact.[82]

Figure 6.3 Detailed (a) and abstract (b) models of the structure of DNA.

transmitted genetic information. These included Linus Pauling at the California Institute of Technology, Rosalind Franklin and Maurice Wilkins at King's College London, and James Watson and Francis Crick at Cambridge University. In 1953, informed by X-ray crystallography data from Franklin, Watson and Crick arrived at one of the most influential results in all of science - the double-helix model of DNA (shown in Figure 6.3).

The connection to one advantageous property of the discrete structure of DNA was immediately apparent to Watson and Crick. In their seminal paper they wrote, "It has not escaped our notice that the specific pairing we have postulated immediately suggests a possible copying mechanism for the genetic material."[83] They were referring to the fact that the double-helix structure enables perfect replication because the DNA can unwind, with each strand serving as a template for synthesizing its complementary strand through the specific base-pairing rules they identified (A with T, G with C). Indeed, soon after Watson and Crick's discovery, experiments showed that DNA duplicates precisely in this manner during cell division, so that each new cell can have its own copy. The discovery of the molecular structure of DNA brought biology into the burgeoning information age, for it demonstrated that written in a four-letter alphabet was the blueprint to life itself.*

Reading the Blueprint

Once it was finally understood that DNA encodes life's blueprints, the next challenge was to uncover how these instructions are read and interpreted. After several years of intense study, in 1957 Francis Crick proposed what he called the central dogma of molecular biology: that information flows from DNA to proteins in one direction and is never transmitted back from proteins.[84] In other words, the information in DNA is used to make proteins, and this transfer of information is strictly one-way. This means that changes acquired by proteins during an organism's lifetime are not written back into DNA or passed on to the next generation.

By the early 1960s, it became clear that DNA does not directly participate in protein synthesis. Instead, this task is delegated to messenger RNA (mRNA), which serves as a temporary copy of a gene's sequence and delivers the genetic information to ribosomes, the molecular factories where proteins are built. The relevant "expressed" parts of DNA are copied in a process called *transcription,* in which protein enzymes read the DNA template

* The entire human genome was sequenced in 2003 as part of the Human Genome Project. This marked a milestone in biology by providing a complete map of the over 20,000 human genes.

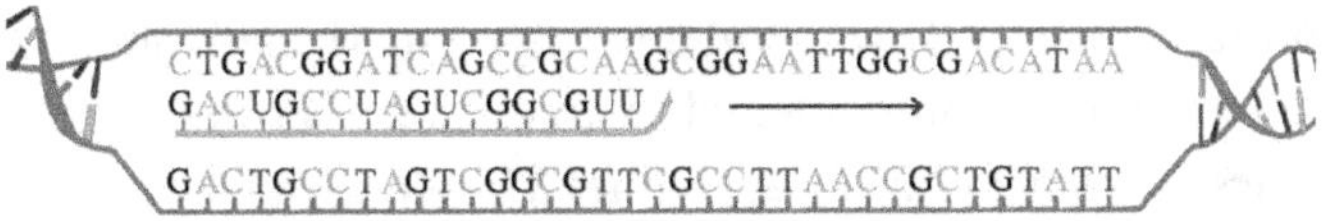

Figure 6.4 An illustration of the process of transcription, in which the unwound DNA double strand serves as a template for synthesizing a complementary RNA strand. The outer strands in the figure represent the DNA, while the inner strand represents the newly formed RNA.[85]

and synthesize an RNA molecule with a complementary sequence. During this process, each base in the DNA strand determines its counterpart in RNA, with uracil in RNA taking the place that thymine occupies in DNA, while the other base pairings remain unchanged. Transcription begins when specific proteins bind to particular regions of DNA, allowing genes to be selectively turned on and off – a principle established in the early 1960s by French scientists François Jacob and Jacques Monod.[86]* Transcription also makes use of error correction, another useful property of the digital nature of DNA. Specialized enzymes perform proofreading to ensure that the mRNA strand contains a faithful copy of the original DNA sequence in the alphabet A, U, G, C (illustrated in Figure 6.4).

Nearly every cell in the human body contains a complete copy of this genetic code, stored in its DNA. The instructions encoded there are used primarily to produce proteins. It may seem surprising, but much of the diversity across species, and even among individuals within a species, ultimately traces back to proteins. These differences arise not only from variations in protein sequences themselves but also, and often more importantly, from differences in *gene expression* – that is, when, where, and how strongly particular genes are expressed. Encoding proteins is therefore one of the most

* Not all genes are active in all cells at all times – a muscle cell uses a different subset of genes than a nerve cell, despite containing identical DNA.

important roles of DNA. Proteins carry out virtually all cellular functions and are fundamental to an organism's physical characteristics and biochemical capabilities.* But this leads to a paradox: ribosomes are made partly of RNA, yet their assembly and function depend on proteins. DNA must therefore contain the instructions for building the very molecular factories that read and interpret its code.

There is a related problem in computer science of creating self-replicating machines. The argument suggesting it is impossible is as follows: For a machine to make an exact copy of itself, it would need to put instructions into the copy of how to reproduce itself, making the copy more complicated than the original. Such skepticism was expressed by people in many forms over time. The eminent philosopher Immanuel Kant expressed it by stating that "one wheel in the watch does not produce another, and still less does one watch produce other watches." And in his 1872 work, *Erewhon; Or, Over the Range*, the English critic Samuel Butler wrote "machines which reproduce machinery do not reproduce machines after their own kind."[88]

Both Kant and Butler, and many other luminaries, knew that life achieves self-reproduction, but they believed this ability marked a fundamental divide between living organisms and machines. But at least for the case of self-reproducibility, they were all proven wrong by the mathematician John von Neumann, who designed such a machine in the late 1940s, demonstrating that self-reproducing machines are indeed possible.[89] As scientists developed a better understanding of biological processes, beliefs in a fundamental divide between living organisms and machines

* A striking insight from modern genomics is that only about two percent of human DNA directly encodes proteins. The rest does not correspond to genes in the usual sense. Some of this noncoding DNA is essential for regulating gene expression. Much of it, however, consists of repetitive sequences with no clearly established biological role, accumulated over evolutionary timescales.[87]

waned, and questions about how proteins carry out their functions took on renewed importance.

Protein Folding and Prediction

Proteins do not emerge from the cell's molecular machinery in their final, functional form. Instead, they begin life as linear chains of amino acids called *polypeptides,* which must fold into precise three-dimensional structures to function properly. These polypeptides are produced during *translation,* the stage of gene expression in which ribosomes read messenger RNA and assemble amino acids in sequence.

A polypeptide must then adopt its proper three-dimensional shape to become a functional protein. The linear sequence of amino acids produced by the ribosome is known as the *primary structure.* Bonds between neighboring segments of the chain give rise to the secondary structure, composed mainly of "alpha helices" and "beta sheets." These elements then fold together into the full three-dimensional configuration of the polypeptide chain, called the *tertiary structure.* In some cases, multiple folded chains further assemble into a *quaternary structure,* forming a fully functioning protein. These stages are illustrated in Figure 6.5.

So, how does protein folding happen in cells? To better understand this process, in 1972, American biochemist Christian Anfinsen performed the following experiment. He isolated a protein called ribonuclease in a test tube and used chemicals to denature, or unfold, it from its three-dimensional shape. Then he removed the denaturing chemicals and discovered that the protein refolded itself back to the same three-dimensional structure it had previously![91] The protein folds itself this way because the folded state is more stable than the unfolded one: It requires less energy to maintain under the physical conditions inside the cell. In other words, when

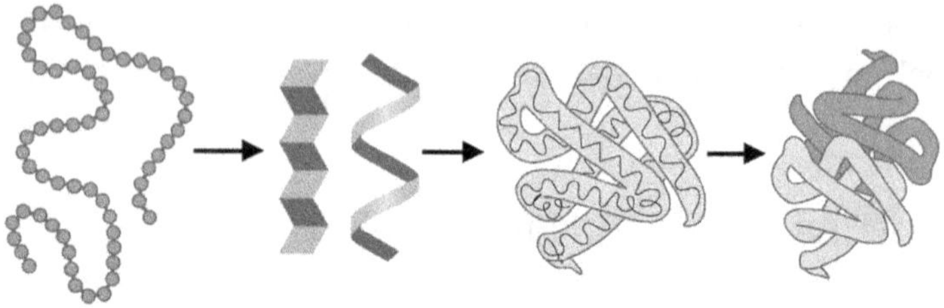

Figure 6.5 An illustration of the amino acid primary structure (left), secondary structure (center left), tertiary structure (center right), and finally the quaternary structure forming the protein (right).[90]

all interactions among the protein, the surrounding water, and thermal motion are taken into account, the folded shape is the one the system naturally settles into.* A major contributor to this stability is the *hydrophobic effect*: Amino acids that repel water tend to cluster together in the interior of the protein, while hydrophilic ones remain exposed on the surface.

Finding the most stable configuration of a polypeptide – the three-dimensional shape it naturally adopts – can also be phrased as a computational problem. From that standpoint, while finding the secondary structure is not difficult, many simplified versions of protein folding have been shown to be NP-complete. This means that there are strong reasons to believe that no efficient algorithm can solve all possible instances of the protein-folding problem (Chapter 4 explains NP-completeness in more detail). Yet nature somehow manages to find these stable configurations both quickly and reliably. This suggests that biologically relevant instances may avoid the cases that give rise to computational difficulty. It is also

* It is worth noting that inside cells, protein folding usually involves assistance from specialized proteins called "chaperones" that help prevent misfolding and improper clumping during the folding process. These chaperones are crucial because misfolded proteins can lead to various diseases, including Alzheimer's and Parkinson's.

possible that evolution has selected sequences that are inherently easier to fold.

Nonetheless, accurately predicting protein structure had for many decades remained one of the greatest challenges in computational biology. Even those sequences that nature could fold with ease gave computers trouble – this problem is comparable to predicting the shape a string of beads will twist into when dropped into a bucket. Traditional algorithms tried to model the physical processes that lead to efficient folding in the real world, but they were time-intensive and produced mixed results. Finally, a breakthrough came in 2018 when a program called `AlphaFold` started outperforming these approaches with a new strategy involving machine learning.[92] `AlphaFold` did not try to simulate the physical processes inside cells but rather used machine learning techniques (Chapter 4 has an explanation of machine learning algorithms) developed in 2016 for playing the game Go and applied them to the protein-folding problem. By 2020, the second version of the program, `AlphaFold2`, was achieving unprecedented levels of accuracy hailed as "transformational" for science.[93]

There are a few important reasons why scientists are so enthusiastic about this advance. A protein's function is determined by its three-dimensional structure, and there are millions of different protein variants across just humans. Only a small fraction of those have been experimentally visualized using X-ray crystallography and other imaging techniques. Being able to understand a protein's shape from just its amino acid sequence dramatically increases scientists' knowledge. But that is only part of the story – by being able to predict the structure of proteins, scientists can invent new polypeptides and quickly determine their protein shape. This has the potential to accelerate the design of new medicines and even has nonmedical applications, for example, new enzymes for breaking down pollutants.

Hacking the Code

While scientists had begun to decode DNA and unravel the mechanisms by which its instructions are read and executed, they faced one fundamental limitation that differentiated biological code from its computational counterpart. Unlike computer code, which programmers can both read and write, the genetic code resisted precise, deliberate modification.

For eons, genetic code had been manipulable only through random mutation, sexual recombination, and natural selection. But beginning in the 1970s, scientists developed the first tools to deliberately modify genetic material. Bacteria naturally produce proteins called restriction enzymes that act like molecular scissors, cutting up unwanted DNA from invading viruses, as well as other proteins called ligases that act to join DNA pieces together. By combining these tools, researchers could move genes from one organism to another, proving that genetic manipulation was possible. These bacterial scissors, however, only cut at specific, predetermined spots scattered throughout the genome, making precise edits nearly impossible. Over time scientists developed more sophisticated tools that could be aimed at chosen targets, but this process was laborious, expensive, and prone to failure.

The situation changed dramatically with the discovery and development of "clustered regularly interspaced short palindromic repeats" (CRISPR) technology, which transformed gene-editing from a laborious craft into a precise and accessible tool that is revolutionizing biology. Like many scientific discoveries, CRISPR began with a puzzle. In the late 1980s, a team of Japanese scientists led by Yoshizumi Ishino noticed repeated DNA sequences in the genome of *E. coli* bacteria, but they were baffled as to their purpose. They concluded their research paper by saying "So far, no sequence homologous to these has been found elsewhere ... and the biological significance of these sequences is not known."[94]

Over time, similar repeated sequences were observed in other bacteria, and in 2002, Dutch microbiologist Ruud Jansen and Spanish researcher Francisco Mojica coined the term CRISPR for these curious repeats. Scientists eventually identified regions of the genome, called CRISPR loci, where these repeated sequences are reliably found. In 2005 multiple research groups independently discovered that these repeated sequences came from the DNA of viruses that reproduce inside bacteria - apparently, the bacteria stored virus DNA inside their genome as a defense mechanism against these viruses. These stored sequences are then transcribed to RNA, which is used by specialized CRISPR-associated (Cas) proteins inside bacteria in a "search and destroy" mission to find the matching viral DNA and cut it.*

This microbial defense system turned out to be a powerful molecular scalpel. Molecular biologists quickly realized that with proper guidance, CRISPR could be used not just to fight viruses in bacteria but to precisely edit any DNA. This potential became a reality in 2012, when American biochemist Jennifer Doudna's and French microbiologist Emmanuelle Charpentier's teams first demonstrated gene editing in a test tube.[95] Then a year later in 2013, groups led by American scientists Feng Zhang and George Church showed how to use CRISPR in living mammalian cells, including making use of natural DNA repair mechanisms to splice the cut strands of DNA back together.[96,97]

CRISPR technology has progressed rapidly since these early breakthroughs. Certain conditions such as sickle cell disease can be treated *ex vivo*, or outside the human body: Blood stem cells are extracted from a patient, the genome of those cells is edited, the cells are multiplied, and finally they are re-infused back into the patient. The edited stem cells then create healthy red blood cells

* There is a safety mechanism in the CRISPR loci to ensure the Cas protein does not destroy the bacterial DNA that contained the original pattern.

in the patient. More recent trials explore treatment *in vivo*, inside the body, by packaging the Cas proteins with guide RNA inside modified viruses and injecting them straight into the tissues that need to be treated.

In principle, CRISPR could do far more than treat disease. It opens the door to human self-modification, engineered species, designer viruses, or virtually any imaginable scenario once biology becomes editable code. Already, CRISPR is being used in agriculture, pest control, and synthetic biology. These applications raise profound questions about what it means to edit life - questions society is only beginning to confront.

Further Explorations

Historical Notes

Beginning with Mendel's early experiments and the Boveri–Sutton theory establishing the foundations of modern genetics, the history of this field involves one astounding intellectual discovery after another. It is therefore not surprising that, like the history of quantum mechanics is full of Nobel Prizes, many of the scientists in this chapter have won Nobel Prizes in physiology, medicine, or chemistry.

- Thomas Hunt Morgan for his discoveries relating to how chromosomes carry hereditary information.
- Linus Pauling for his work on the nature of chemical bonds. This predated his involvement in finding the molecular structure of DNA, but it heavily influenced Watson and Crick's later discoveries.
- Alfred Hershey for his work definitively showing that DNA and not protein carries genetic information.
- Francis Crick, James Watson, and Maurice Wilkins for their discoveries related to the molecular structure of DNA.

- François Jacob and Jacques Monod for discovering how cells regulate the use of their genes.
- Christian Anfinsen for his work on the protein ribonuclease refolding itself after being denatured.
- Demis Hassabis and John M. Jumper for their contributions to protein structure prediction with `AlphaFold` and its later variants.
- Emmanuelle Charpentier and Jennifer Doudna for their work on developing CRISPR technology.

The above list is also conspicuous in whom it omits, reinforcing the limitation of judging the merit of works by prizes alone. It also omits Nobel Prize winners in molecular biology whose work was not covered in this chapter.

Many scientists believe that the paper of Oswald Avery, Colin MacLeod, and Maclyn McCarty showing that DNA, and not protein, stores genetic information was among the most influential scientific works never to win a Nobel Prize. Rosalind Franklin is mentioned as a key figure in the description of the prize given to Francis Crick, James Watson, and Maurice Wilkins, but she was deceased by the time the award was given. Controversially, Alfred Hershey's junior co-author, Martha Chase, did not share in the prize. Francisco Mojica was also greatly involved in advancing gene editing technologies and is considered an "unsung hero" of CRISPR.

For the Mathematically Inclined

The idea developed in this section dates back at least to the physicist George Gamow, who argued on mathematical grounds that a triplet code was the minimal viable encoding scheme for proteins – an idea later confirmed by experiments.[98]

The manner in which ribosomes process mRNA is interesting: mRNA is read in codons, which are groups of three nucleotides from `A`, `U`, `G`, `C`. Each codon encodes a different *amino acid*, the molecules out of which proteins are built. Ribosomes can

Table 6.6 Codons grouped by their first and second base (rows) and third base (columns). Resulting amino acids are shaded in a unique light gray for visibility. The start and stop codons indicate when to start and stop synthesis, respectively.

1st+2nd	U	C	A	G
UU	Phe	Phe	Leu	Leu
UC	Ser	Ser	Ser	Ser
UA	Tyr	Tyr	**Stop**	**Stop**
UG	Cys	Cys	**Stop**	Trp
CU	Leu	Leu	Leu	Leu
CC	Pro	Pro	Pro	Pro
CA	His	His	Gln	Gln
CG	Arg	Arg	Arg	Arg
AU	Ile	Ile	Ile	Met/**Start**
AC	Thr	Thr	Thr	Thr
AA	Asn	Asn	Lys	Lys
AG	Ser	Ser	Arg	Arg
GU	Val	Val	Val	Val
GC	Ala	Ala	Ala	Ala
GA	Asp	Asp	Glu	Glu
GG	Gly	Gly	Gly	Gly

synthesize proteins from the following 20 different amino acids: Alanine (Ala), Arginine (Arg), Asparagine (Asn), Aspartic acid (Asp), Cysteine (Cys), Glutamic acid (Glu), Glutamine (Gln), Glycine (Gly), Histidine (His), Isoleucine (Ile), Leucine (Leu), Lysine (Lys), Methionine (Met), Phenylalanine (Phe), Proline (Pro), Serine (Ser), Threonine (Thr), Tryptophan (Trp), Tyrosine (Tyr), and Valine (Val).

Codons therefore need to be at least three nucleotides long; two would not have been enough to encode all 20 possibilities (since $4^2 = 16$). Three nucleotides are enough to encode approximately $4^3 = 64$ different codons, but since proteins are built from only 20 amino acids, multiple similar codons usually map to the same amino acid. For example GGU, GGC, GGA, and GGG all map to the amino acid glycine, making it resilient to an error in the last nucleotide. The full mapping from codons to amino acids is summarized in Table 6.6.

Mutations that change one base but not the amino acid are common, especially when the mutation is in the third codon position, which is sometimes called the "wobble" position. For many amino acids, changing the third base doesn't change the outcome, meaning that errors are often "silent." This serves as a mild form of error correction, illustrating yet another link between molecular biology and information theory.

Additional Reading

James Watson's well-known book *The Double Helix* contains his fascinating personal (and controversial) account of the discovery of the structure of DNA. For a more sweeping view of the field, the book *The Gene: An Intimate History* by doctor and biologist Siddhartha Mukherjee tells a comprehensive and detailed history of genetics from Mendel to CRISPR, intertwined with his own personal story.

7

The Logic of Life
Game Theory

The theory of evolution, now widely understood and taught in schools throughout the world, was a revolutionary idea and perhaps the most profound discovery of the nineteenth century. It shed light on a multitude of phenomena and changed the way the entire field of biology is interpreted. The eminent geneticist Theodosius Dobzhansky wrote a famous essay that made this point, with the title "Nothing in biology makes sense except in the light of evolution."[99] Yet, this insight tells only part of the story. Over time, it has become apparent that a full understanding of evolution depends on a grasp of *game theory*. Organisms don't merely adapt to their environment - they adapt to each other in an ongoing strategic interaction. Evolution is not simply a struggle with nature; it is, fundamentally, a strategic game, with rules that govern the strategies and payoffs of organisms.

Figure 7.1 Image of a painting of Nefertari playing the game senet.[100]

This more encompassing view of game theory, which applies beyond the narrow study of rational decision making, is not as widely accepted or understood. Recognizing that game theory can illuminate problems outside its traditional setting is among the great insights of the twentieth century. Game theory extends to far more than biological evolution: It helps explain why cooperation can emerge among selfish individuals, why conflict often persists even when everyone loses, and how surprisingly simple strategies can sustain cooperation over time.

Zero-Sum Games

Game theory involves the study of structured interactions among players whose *payoffs* (outcomes) depend on both their actions and those of the other players. These interactions can be turn-based like tic-tac-toe or simultaneous-action like rock-paper-scissors; they might involve only two players or many more; they might involve chance like poker or be deterministic like chess, where nothing is left to chance, and so on. While turn-based games have been played at least since the times of Ancient Egypt (as shown in Figure 7.1) and

Table 7.2 Payoff matrix for rock-paper-scissors.

Player 1 \ player 2	Rock	Paper	Scissors
Rock	(0,0)	(−1,1)	(1,−1)
Paper	(1,−1)	(0,0)	(−1,1)
Scissors	(−1,1)	(1,−1)	(0,0)

chess has been studied for over a millennium,[101] their analysis usually boils down to figuring out the "best" move regardless of the opponent's strategy.

Modern game theory began with the 1928 work of the brilliant Hungarian–American mathematician John von Neumann, who proved what is now known as the *minimax theorem.*[102] His theorem applied to the specific case of two-player zero-sum simultaneous games. In a *zero-sum game,* one player's gain always comes at the expense of the other player's loss. Von Neumann showed that in these special games, when each player has a finite number of actions, there exists an optimal strategy for each player that minimizes his worst-case loss on average, or equivalently, maximizes his guaranteed gain on average. When the players play their optimal strategies, the game reaches its *game value,* the average amount that player 1 wins and player 2 loses.

A familiar example of such a game is rock-paper-scissors. When analyzing a game, it can be helpful to organize the payoffs to the two players in a table called a *payoff matrix.* A payoff matrix illustrates the outcomes when different pairs of actions are played by the two players. The first player chooses an action from the rows and the second player from among the columns. The corresponding cell shows the payoffs to the first and second player, respectively. Table 7.2 shows the rock-paper-scissors payoff matrix. One can check that this game is zero-sum because the two entries in each cell sum to zero.

In rock-paper-scissors, the optimal strategy for each player is to act randomly; strategies that use randomness are called *mixed strategies* because they "mix" different actions with probabilities (strategies that take one action deterministically are called *pure*). Always playing one action cannot be a good idea, but playing each of the three actions of rock, paper, and scissors with equal probability is optimal. The expected payoff in that case will be zero, making zero the game value for this game.*

What von Neumann was able to show is that this fact holds true more generally for optimal strategies in any zero-sum game. When one player plays an optimal strategy, the opponent cannot improve his expected payoff by responding optimally; all best responses lead to the same outcome, the game value. Once this happens, neither player can take advantage of the other. An intriguing real-world example involves penalty kicks in soccer (a zero-sum game). Evidence indicates that the distribution of where players aim and where goalies dive approaches the optimal strategies of both players.[103]

Nash's Revolution

The field of game theory saw continual advances after von Neumann's seminal work until the American mathematician John Nash revolutionized the field in 1950. As a graduate student, he wrote a short paper showing that the minimax theorem has a natural counterpart in general-sum multiplayer games. In particular, he proved that every game in which each player has a finite number

* The game value is not zero for all zero-sum games. For example, if the payoff matrix in Table 7.2 is modified so that all the (0,0) entries are changed to (−1,1) (i.e., ties go to the second player), the game value would become −1/3, which means that the second player would gain 1/3 from the first player on average when both play optimally.

Table 7.3 Payoff matrix for battle of the sexes.

Woman\man	Opera	Football
Opera	(2,1)	(0,0)
Football	(0,0)	(1,2)

of actions has a stable set of mixed strategies. When players use these strategies, no one can do better by changing his behavior on his own. These *Nash equilibrium* strategies have the property that when all players play according to them, no player has an incentive to deviate on his own. The idea is that once players arrive at these strategies, they have no reason to change their behavior afterwards, and his astounding result showed that every such game has at least one such equilibrium![104]

An example of a general-sum game is battle of the sexes, which was introduced in 1957 by American academics Robert Duncan Luce and Howard Raiffa.[105] Its payoffs are shown in Table 7.3. The traditional story behind this game is that player 1 is a woman and player 2 is a man, and they each need to decide whether to go to the opera or to a football game after work. The two want to spend time with each other, so if they go to different events, both their payoffs will be zero. If they both go to the opera, both will have a positive payoff, but the woman's will be higher, whereas the man's will be higher if they both go to the football game. This game has three distinct Nash equilibria: (1) both players always going to the opera, (2) both players always going to the football game, and (3) both players acting according to the mixed strategies given in Table 7.4.

When these mixed strategies are used, the expected payoff for each of the two players is 2/3.* No player can improve his payoff

* The calculation follows for player 1. With probability 2/9, they meet at the opera and she gets a payoff of 2. With probability 2/9, they meet at the football game

Table 7.4 A mixed strategy Nash equilibrium for battle of the sexes

Woman	Man
Opera with probability 2/3	Opera with probability 1/3
Football with probability 1/3	Football with probability 2/3

by changing his behavior on his own, which is precisely why these strategies form a Nash equilibrium. Although this outcome treats the two players symmetrically, it leaves both worse off than the equilibria in which they successfully coordinate on either the opera or the football game.

This example highlights a key feature of general-sum games. Unlike zero-sum games, they do not necessarily have a single pair of optimal strategies or a single game value. Instead, they may admit multiple equilibria, each leading to a different outcome. Nash's theorem guarantees only that at least one such stable outcome exists. It also explains why not every reasonable-looking strategy profile qualifies as an equilibrium. For example, if both players were to randomize evenly between opera and football, they would each earn a higher expected payoff of 3/4. Yet this outcome is unstable: Player 1 could improve her payoff by always choosing the opera and player 2 by always choosing football. Because each has an incentive to deviate, this strategy pair is not a Nash equilibrium.

Examples like this also reveal a limitation of one-shot games. Nash equilibrium captures stability at a single moment, but many of the most important social behaviors, especially cooperation, can emerge through repeated interaction over time.

and she gets payoff of 1. Otherwise she gets 0. In expectation, she gets $(2/9) \times 2 + (2/9) \times 1 = 2/3$. If she instead decides to change her strategy and always go to the opera, her expected payoff would remain 2/3 (she would receive a payoff of 2 with probability 1/3), and if she were to always go to the football game, her payoff would again be 2/3 (she would receive a payoff of 1 with probability 2/3). She therefore has no incentive to switch strategies. The same calculation, swapping opera and football, holds for player 2.

Table 7.5 Payoff matrix for prisoner's dilemma.

Prisoner 1\prisoner 2	Cooperate	Defect
Cooperate	(−1,−1)	(−5,0)
Defect	(0,−5)	(−4,−4)

Repeated Games and Cooperation

Nash equilibria quickly became an important object of study for scientists and policymakers alike. It seemed reasonable to assume that players engaged in strategic interactions in the real world would eventually arrive at such stable outcomes. During the Cold War, this assumption took on particular urgency. The United States and the Soviet Union faced repeated strategic decisions about whether to cooperate by seeking peace or to defect by escalating conflict, including the potential use of nuclear weapons. In the 1950s, one of the many groups thinking carefully about these questions was the RAND Corporation, a think tank that advised US policymakers on strategic and military planning. In this context, and as part of a broader effort to understand strategic interaction, RAND mathematicians Merrill Flood and Melvin Dresher introduced what became known as the prisoner's dilemma.[106*]

The prisoner's dilemma derives its name from a hypothetical situation where two coconspirators, who each want to serve as little time in prison as possible, have a chance to defect against the other (by confessing) or cooperate (by staying silent). The payoffs for their possible actions are given in Table 7.5. If both cooperate, they will each get a year in prison on a lesser charge. If one cooperates and one defects, the cooperating player will be convicted of a larger crime and go to prison for five years, and the defector will get his

* The name "prisoner's dilemma" came later from mathematician Albert W. Tucker.

year sentence forgiven and go free. Finally, if both defect, they will both be convicted of the larger crime but also get a year off for telling, so they both will go to prison for four years.

Defecting is always individually better for each player than cooperating, regardless of what the other player does. The "dilemma" is the conflict between individual rationality, which leads to both players defecting and serving four years, and collective benefit, where both players should cooperate and serve one. Regrettably for both players, the prisoner's dilemma has only one Nash equilibrium, where both players defect.

But when Flood and Dresher invited their colleagues, economist Armen Alchian and mathematician John Williams, to play the game for a hundred rounds,* something unexpected happened. Even though the two players clearly understood that defecting was optimal in any given round, Alchian and Williams cooperated for 60 of the rounds![107] It appeared that cooperation could somehow come about when a game is *iterated*, played repeatedly. This behavior posed a puzzle: Standard game theory predicted persistent defection, yet repeated interaction seemed to allow cooperation to emerge. As a result, repeated games became an object of intense scientific interest. In the following years, economists and mathematicians showed that cooperation can indeed be sustained in iterated prisoner's dilemma and related games, most notably through work by Robert Aumann.[108] By the 1960s and 1970s, the idea that cooperation could arise from long-term interaction was widely accepted.

Then, in 1980, University of Michigan political scientist Robert Axelrod ran a tournament to systematically test various strategies for the iterated prisoner's dilemma. Axelrod invited well-known experts across a wide variety of disciplines to submit computer

* One can, for example, add 5 to all entries in Table 7.5 without changing anything fundamental about the game and pay each player his corresponding entry on every round.

programs that would be played against each other for an unknown number of rounds. Every submitted program played against every other program, and the winner was the program that did the best overall.[109]

The competitors entered many different programs, including a program that always cooperated (it did well with other cooperators), "always defect" (it was in Nash equilibrium with itself), and a plethora of very sophisticated strategies explicitly made to exploit weaknesses in their opponents. The winning entry, however, turned out to be nothing at all complicated. Anatol Rapoport, a mathematical psychologist with very diverse interests, submitted the following four-line Fortran program (shown expanded in Algorithm 7.6) that he called TIT-FOR-TAT.[110]

```
program TIT-FOR-TAT()
    cooperate on the first move
    for each subsequent round:
        if opponent cooperated in the previous round, then
            cooperate
        else (if opponent defected in the previous round)
            defect
end program
```

Algorithm 7.6: TIT-FOR-TAT.

The algorithm TIT-FOR-TAT begins by cooperating on the first round and then proceeds to do whatever its opponent did on the previous round. Rapoport appealed to insights into human nature to develop a simple yet powerful program that follows these common-sense principles: (1) start out by being nice, (2) prevent being taken advantage of, but also (3) be forgiving. After announcing the results of the tournament and the winning program, Axelrod ran a second tournament, which had submissions that were created to take advantage of `TIT-FOR-TAT`'s reciprocity. But those programs did not do well against each other, and `TIT-FOR-TAT` won again![111]

Game theorists have since analyzed the `TIT-FOR-TAT` strategy in particular to learn why it is so effective. It turns out that `TIT-FOR-TAT` can indeed be in Nash equilibrium against itself and also against many other strategy profiles in iterated prisoner's dilemma, so long as their future payoffs were sufficiently valued or there was enough uncertainty in the number of rounds still to play. But unlike the program that always defects and many others, `TIT-FOR-TAT` gets a higher average payoff in equilibrium.[112]

This helps explain why people have adopted norms to help other cooperators and to punish defectors. Neighbors will help each other without immediate benefit in part because they may need help later in return. Reciprocity is also observed in animals. Among the many examples are vampire bats sharing blood meals with other bats who have shared in the past[113] and pied flycatchers protecting those fellow birds who have previously protected others from predators.[114] This equilibrium is better for a group overall than an equilibrium in which each member only looks out for himself.

Evolving Better Equilibria

A related question that naturally arises is how an equilibrium can evolve in a population in the first place, and which equilibria might be displaced by other better equilibria. A formal study of what strategies can evolve was started by the British mathematical evolutionary biologist John Maynard Smith in the 1970s. Smith and his colleague George Price introduced a simple model to study how strategies can evolve when animals of a single species compete over resources. They modeled this interaction as a single-round simultaneous game in which animals adopt one of two strategies: "hawks" (fighters) or "doves" (sharers).[115] When a resource of some value,

Table 7.7 The hawk–dove game payoff matrix.

Player 1\player 2	Hawk	Dove
Hawk	(−2,−2)	(6,0)
Dove	(0,6)	(3,3)

say 6, is found in the presence of two animals, their interaction will depend on the animals' willingness to share or fight. When two doves meet, they will share it and each get a payoff of 3. If a hawk and a dove meet, the hawk will take the food for himself and get payoff 6, leaving the dove with nothing. If two hawks meet, they end up fighting and each get a loss, say −2. Table 7.7 gives the payoff matrix for these values.

Smith and Price defined the notion of an *evolutionarily stable strategy* as one that, when adopted by most of the population, cannot be invaded; that is, a small number of "mutant" individuals playing a different strategy cannot earn higher payoffs and therefore cannot spread. While every evolutionarily stable strategy is a Nash equilibrium of the underlying game, the converse is not true: Games often have Nash equilibria that are stable against individual deviations but fragile under evolutionary invasion.

The hawk–dove game provides a simple example of how evolutionary considerations can single out a stable population mix, even when individual behavior is modeled as a one-shot game. In a population of all hawks, a dove mutation can invade and get a better expected outcome since most hawks would meet other hawks and get −2 on average, whereas a dove would get 0 against hawks. Similarly, in a population of doves invaded by hawks, doves would get 3 on average, whereas hawks would get 6. Neither of these populations would be evolutionarily stable. But a population of 60% hawks and 40% doves would be stable. Hawks would meet other hawks 60% of the time and get −2 and meet doves 40% of the time and get 6, yielding an average payoff of $.6\times(-2)+.4\times6=1.2$. Doves, on the other hand, would get nothing 60% of the time and 40% of the time get 3, which also averages to 1.2. This population mix is evolutionarily stable and cannot be invaded.

This simple hawk and dove game offers some insights into more realistic repeated games like iterated prisoner's dilemma. A population playing this game in which all players always defect is not evolutionarily stable and can end up being overtaken by a mutation that introduces reciprocal cooperation (e.g., `TIT-FOR-TAT`). The reason is that reciprocal cooperation performs about as well as defectors against other defectors, but two reciprocal cooperators do significantly better against each other because mutual cooperation yields a higher payoff than mutual defection. As reciprocal cooperators grow in the population, their strategy becomes more and more advantageous as they meet each other more frequently, leading to their eventual dominance. This model provides one of the most convincing accounts of how sustained cooperation can evolve.[116]

The evolutionary and repeated-game models discussed herein explain how stable patterns of behavior can arise from simple strategic interactions – how equilibrium can emerge, persist, and spread through a population. But these ideas extend well beyond the small-scale settings in which they were first developed.

Modern economists and engineers now use game-theoretic reasoning not merely to analyze behavior but to design systems in which desirable outcomes emerge from strategic interaction. When governments auction radio spectrum to telecommunications companies, the rules are crafted so that bidders reveal their true valuations and resources flow to those who value them most.[117] Traffic engineers model congestion as a game in which each driver chooses the fastest route, and the resulting equilibria often mirror the inefficiency of the prisoner's dilemma.[118] Understanding these dynamics has led to interventions, such as congestion pricing, that reshape incentives and improve collective outcomes.[119] Even recent successes such as AI systems achieving superhuman performance in poker rely on ideas first illustrated in simple settings,[120] ideas that now underpin much of modern strategic reasoning.

Further Explorations

Historical Notes

The origins of modern game theory date back to correspondence between mathematicians Blaise Pascal and Pierre de Fermat in the mid-seventeenth century. Their work laid the foundations of probability theory, which would later become central to game-theoretic reasoning. Pascal also developed the philosophical argument known as Pascal's wager, an early attempt to reason formally about decision making under uncertainty. In the mid-eighteenth century, Daniel Bernoulli introduced the concept of expected utility as the quantity to be maximized in rational decision making. The numerical payoffs used in game theory are meant to represent such utilities, capturing the outcomes that players ultimately care about.

Several key ideas underlying modern game theory appeared well before the field was formally defined. In the early eighteenth century, the politician and diplomat James Waldegrave analyzed a French two-player card game called *le Her*. He identified an optimal strategy in what is now recognized as the first recorded example of a minimax mixed strategy. In the nineteenth century, the philosopher and economist Antoine Augustin Cournot analyzed strategic interaction in a duopoly, identifying what would later be recognized as pure-strategy equilibria and anticipating Nash's general equilibrium concept.

In the early twentieth century, these strands began to coalesce into a mathematical theory. The French mathematician Émile Borel studied strategic play in finite games and emphasized the role of mixed strategies, developing several special cases of minimax reasoning. Building on this line of work, John von Neumann proved the minimax theorem in 1928, establishing the existence of optimal strategies in two-player zero-sum games. In 1944, von Neumann and Oskar Morgenstern published *Theory of Games and Economic Behavior*, which introduced game theory as a unified mathematical framework and firmly embedded Bernoulli's notion of expected utility into its foundations.

The next major advance came in 1950, when John Nash defined what is now called Nash equilibrium and showed that every finite game admits at least one such stable outcome. Nash's result extended von Neumann's work beyond zero-sum games to arbitrary strategic interactions, dramatically broadening the scope of game theory.

Subsequent developments refined and extended these ideas. In the 1960s, Reinhard Selten introduced subgame-perfect equilibria, enabling more precise analysis of sequential and repeated games, while John Harsanyi developed the theory of Bayesian games, allowing for incomplete information. Around the same time, Thomas Schelling applied game-theoretic reasoning to real-world conflict and coordination problems, most notably nuclear brinkmanship. His work helped shape how strategic reasoning about nuclear conflict entered the public imagination, including through cultural portrayals such as Stanley Kubrick's film *Dr. Strangelove.*

In the 1970s and 1980s, evolutionary biologists and social scientists contributed new concepts to game theory. John Maynard Smith introduced evolutionary game theory and the concept of evolutionarily stable strategies, applying strategic reasoning to biological populations rather than rational agents. Around the same time, Robert Axelrod's work on repeated games demonstrated how cooperation can emerge and persist through strategic interaction.

Several of the figures mentioned in this chapter were awarded the Nobel Memorial Prize in Economic Sciences for their contributions, including Robert Aumann, John Harsanyi, John Nash, Thomas Schelling, and Reinhard Selten.

For the Mathematically Inclined

One of John Nash's central contributions to game theory was his proof that every finite strategic game admits a Nash equilibrium. This result – one of the achievements for which he later received a Nobel Memorial Prize in Economic Sciences – rests on a strikingly simple fixed-point idea, whose essential features are outlined here.

A game with n players is described as follows. For each player i, S_i denotes the finite set of pure strategies available to that player, and

$$u_i : S_1 \times \cdots \times S_n \to \mathbb{R}$$

gives player i's payoff for each combination of pure strategies. These payoffs extend naturally to mixed strategies by taking expectations. A *mixed strategy* for player i is a probability distribution over S_i, and the set of all such distributions is written Δ_i.

Each set Δ_i has two key mathematical properties. It is *convex*: Randomizing between two mixed strategies produces another valid mixed strategy. It is also *compact*: It is closed and bounded, so that limits of valid strategies remain valid.

A complete specification of behavior in the game corresponds to a point in the "product space"

$$\Delta = \Delta_1 \times \cdots \times \Delta_n,$$

whose elements represent independently chosen mixed strategies for all players. Because compactness and convexity are preserved under finite products, Δ is itself a compact, convex subset of a finite-dimensional Euclidean space.

Nash's insight was to consider a rule that smoothly adjusts each player's strategy in the direction of better-performing actions. Let

$$\sigma = (\sigma_1, \ldots, \sigma_n) \in \Delta$$

denote a mixed-strategy profile, and let σ_{-i} represent the strategies of all players other than player i. For a pure strategy $s \in S_i$, the quantity $u_i(s, \sigma_{-i})$ is the expected payoff to player i from playing s against the others' mixed strategies.

Associated with each profile σ is a nonnegative vector $v_i(\sigma)$, indexed by pure strategies in S_i, whose components are given by

$$v_i(\sigma)(s) = \max\big(u_i(s, \sigma_{-i}) - u_i(\sigma_i, \sigma_{-i}),\, 0\big).$$

Positive entries correspond precisely to strategies that outperform the player's current mixture, while zero entries indicate strategies that do not. The vector $v_i(\sigma)$ therefore measures how strongly alternative actions "pull" relative to the status quo.

An updated mixed strategy is obtained by increasing the weight on better-performing actions and then normalizing (rescaling) so that total probability remains equal to one:

$$F_i(\sigma) = \text{normalize}[\sigma_i + v_i(\sigma)]\,.$$

Because σ_i is already a probability distribution and $v_i(\sigma)$ is nonnegative, this procedure always produces another valid mixed strategy.

Applying this adjustment rule simultaneously to all players yields a function

$$F(\sigma) = (F_1(\sigma), \ldots, F_n(\sigma)),$$

which maps the strategy space Δ into itself. Each step in the construction – forming expected payoffs, comparing performance, and renormalizing probabilities – is continuous. As a result, the overall mapping F is continuous.

Brouwer's fixed point theorem now applies. This theorem guarantees that any continuous function from a compact convex set to itself has at least one fixed point. Consequently, there exists a mixed-strategy profile $\sigma^* \in \Delta$ for which

$$F(\sigma^*) = \sigma^*.$$

At such a fixed point, the adjustment rule leaves every player's strategy unchanged. Intuitively, this can occur only if no player has any incentive to shift probability toward a different action. Any pure strategy yielding a strictly higher expected payoff would attract additional weight under the adjustment rule, preventing the profile from remaining fixed.

Thus, at a fixed point, every strategy that receives positive probability performs at least as well as any available alternative against the others' strategies. In behavioral terms, each player is already responding optimally to the behavior of the others. This is precisely the defining condition of a mixed-strategy Nash equilibrium.

Additional Reading

An engrossing historical work is *Prisoner's Dilemma: John von Neumann, Game Theory, and the Puzzle of the Bomb*[107] by author William Poundstone. It has fascinating details about game theory's development and its insights into the Cold War. Another excellent book, though not explicitly about game theory but which uses game-theoretic insights throughout, is *The Red Queen: Sex and the Evolution of Human Nature*[121] by science writer Matt Ridley. This book offers many stunning mathematical insights into evolutionary biology.

8

From Stars to Cells
The Carbon Cycle

Carbon has an entire field, organic chemistry, devoted to its study. No other element can boast such a privilege, and for good reason. The distinguished English physicist and astronomer James Jeans observed, "Life exists ... only because the carbon atom possesses certain exceptional properties."[122] Indeed, at the very heart of carbon's remarkable versatility lies an elegant observation: Carbon's unique atomic structure is precisely what enables its astonishingly diverse behavior. Not only does carbon form the basis for all life on Earth, but it also serves a variety of other vital functions. The *carbon cycle* – the movement of carbon across lands, oceans, the atmosphere, living organisms, and Earth's interior – tells a story of interconnectedness that reaches from Earth all the way to distant stars.

The Sixth Element

"We are made of star-stuff," wrote American astronomer and science popularizer Carl Sagan.[123] This popular quote refers to the fact that almost all of the heavier atoms found on Earth, and indeed in the universe, were created in the stars. This seems like a fantastical claim, but it is true. Immediately after the Big Bang, the early universe was composed mostly of hydrogen, which has only one proton. The number of protons in an atom largely determines its chemical properties and is called its *atomic number*, which is sometimes represented by the variable Z. Carbon, for example, has an atomic number of 6, making it the sixth element in the periodic table. All elements not present in the early universe (including carbon) were created through a process of combining lighter atoms - those with smaller atomic numbers - called *nuclear fusion*.

Nuclear fusion is a process that requires extreme pressures and temperatures. For the first few minutes after the Big Bang, the early universe was so hot and dense that elements like helium (atomic number 2) were created. After that, when the universe cooled and stars formed, their cores became the main incubators for fusion. A star exists in a continual struggle against gravity: Gravity constantly pulls matter inward, driving the star toward collapse, while energy released by nuclear fusion pushes outward and keeps the star stable. It is this balance that allows stars to shine.

In stellar cores, fusion produces elements such as carbon, oxygen, and others up to atomic number 26 (iron) in a process known as *stellar nucleosynthesis*.* When fusion creates iron or lighter elements, it releases more energy than it consumes, supplying the energy that counteracts gravity and powers the star.

* Unlike lighter elements, which release more energy than they consume during fusion, heavier elements release more energy net when splitting into lighter ones in a process called fission.

Elements heavier than iron, therefore, are not typically produced in stellar nucleosynthesis. When massive stars exhaust their supply of lighter elements for fusion, the outward support provided by fusion weakens, gravity wins, and the star collapses. This collapse triggers a *supernova* explosion, a process so energetic that it produces elements heavier than iron and ejects newly formed heavy elements, while also dispersing large amounts of carbon synthesized earlier in the star's life throughout space.* Over time, clouds of these heavier elements are coalesced by gravity to form planetary systems, including the solar system. Once distributed throughout Earth, carbon's remarkable flexibility proved crucial to the development of life.

Carbon possesses several remarkable properties that make it exceptionally useful for life and for complex chemistry more broadly. Carbon has four electrons in its outermost shell (illustrated in Figure 8.1a), which it can share with other atoms to form *covalent bonds*. This allows carbon to form complex molecules, including organic compounds. Carbon can bind to itself in chains and rings (forming "cyclic compounds"), facilitating the formation of complex organic molecules, and these bonds are strong and stable (shown in Figure 8.1b for an example). Carbon can also bind to a variety of other elements, again suitable for forming a variety of compounds that are crucial to life. Carbon has other useful properties: It can exist in multiple structural forms called "allotropes" - such as diamond, graphite, and fullerenes, each with notably different physical properties despite being composed of the same element. Carbon atoms can also "hybridize" their electron orbitals, allowing them to form different types of bonds with varying geometries and strengths.

* Another source for the production of heavier elements is the merger of neutron stars, the extremely dense remnants of massive stars.

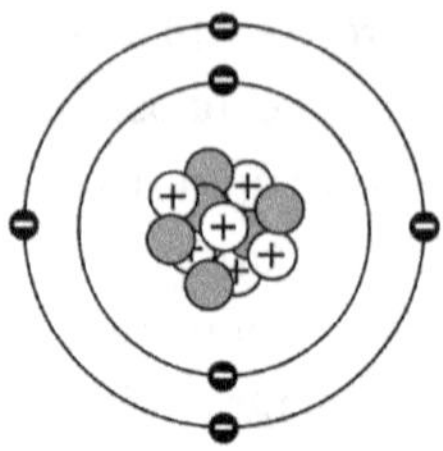

(a) A diagram of the carbon atom, showing six protons (white), neutrons (gray), and electrons (black). Its four valence electrons occupy the outer shell and enable carbon to form bonds with other atoms.

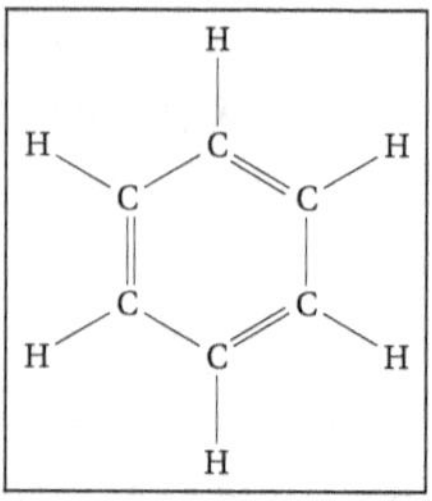

(b) A diagram of a benzene ring, a simple ring-shaped carbon molecule, which is made of six carbon (C) and six hydrogen (H) atoms. The lines represent covalent bonds (the double lines are double bonds).

Figure 8.1 A carbon atom and a carbon ring.

These facets of carbon, many of which were not understood until the twentieth century through techniques such as X-ray crystallography, allow for the formation of large, stable, and chemically versatile molecules. Such molecules are essential for life: They can store information, form structural components of cells, and participate in controlled chemical reactions. This unique combination of stability and flexibility is what allows carbon-based chemistry to support living systems and to enable the carbon cycle.

Photosynthesis

The carbon cycle is the process by which carbon atoms move through the Earth, its atmosphere, and the life that lives on it. Although scientists continually learn more about the carbon cycle, one of its principal components, *photosynthesis*, began to be understood by scientists in the late 1700s.

Photosynthesis is the process by which plants and other organisms such as cyanobacteria (blue-green algae) convert sunlight into chemical energy to fuel their growth. Children often first encounter the concept of photosynthesis in elementary school, but its importance remains underappreciated. The Sun provides the energy for all life on Earth, but as solar panel engineers are acutely aware, harnessing the Sun's energy is not straightforward. Photosynthesis accounts for the vast majority of how the Sun's energy is harnessed by life on Earth. The rest of the creatures, like humans, rely on consuming the byproducts of photosynthesis for their energy via the food chain. But it is photosynthesis that makes complex life possible.

In plants, part of the photosynthesis process uses a specialized pigment called *chlorophyll*, whose molecular structure is believed to have evolved to absorb the red and blue wavelengths from sunlight and convert them to chemical energy.[124] There are still debates among scientists about whether these particular wavelengths are optimal for absorption, but the abundance of chlorophyll in plants explains why their leaves are green: Chlorophyll absorbs mostly red and blue light and reflects green light. It is this reflected light that gives the leaves their green appearance.

In the carbon cycle, carbon dioxide (CO_2) is taken from the atmosphere; its carbon is incorporated, together with hydrogen from water in the soil, into the body of the plant itself through a process known as the Calvin cycle, while oxygen is released. This basic picture is given in Figure 8.2.

Consumption, Respiration, and Release

Animals, like plants, need carbon to make up their cells. Since animals are generally unable to perform photosynthesis, their

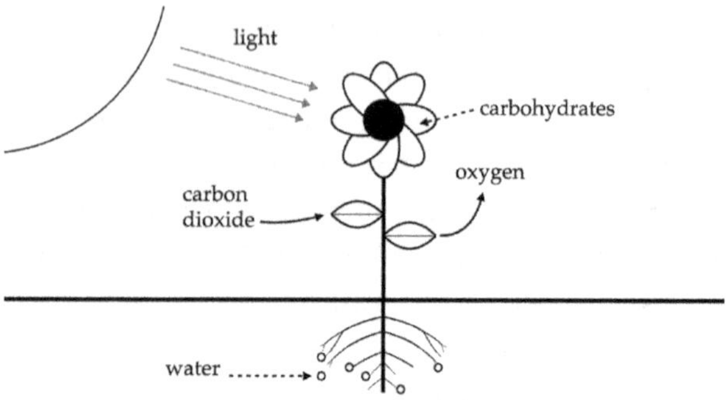

Figure 8.2 An illustration of the inputs and outputs of photosynthesis.[125]

carbon comes mainly from the consumption of food through the food chain. Animals consume plants and/or other animals and incorporate the carbon consumed into their own bodies through complicated metabolic processes. Metabolism is incredibly complicated and still far from fully understood. Figure 8.3 illustrates just the primary human metabolic pathways.

Carbon issues from animals in multiple ways. One, of course, is in feces, especially in undigested material. But, perhaps surprisingly, more carbon is released through cellular *respiration* and exhaled as CO_2. In this process, cells use oxygen to extract energy from carbohydrates. The energy, originally captured during photosynthesis, is thus returned to the organism to power its cells.

This has an unexpected consequence: Animals, including people, lose weight primarily through breathing. The carbon atoms are released during respiration, and this is also how one loses weight by exercising: Working out increases the rate of respiration, which releases carbon faster. A person who tries to "cheat" and breathe fast without doing a commensurate amount of exercise may lose consciousness due to hypocapnia (abnormally low CO_2 levels in

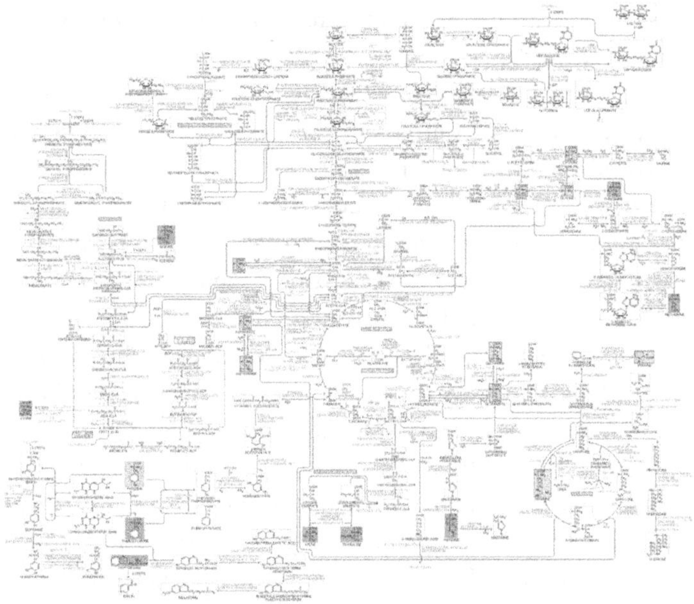

Figure 8.3 A diagram demonstrating the complexity of the primary metabolic pathways in humans. Carbon moves through countless biochemical transformations. No simple chemical equation can describe human metabolism.[126]

the blood), while a person who exercises generates additional CO_2 through increased metabolic activity, allowing faster breathing without dangerous reductions in blood CO_2.*

It is also worth noting that plants and animals can be consumed by bacteria and fungi, and that energy-generating process also releases carbon back into the atmosphere. The carbon stored by plants can also be emitted by other means. For example, when wood is burned, energy originally captured from sunlight during photosynthesis is released as heat, and the carbon that had

* Plant cells also go through respiration, but their released carbon dioxide is immediately reabsorbed in photosynthesis when sufficient light is present to power the reaction.

been locked into plant matter is returned to the atmosphere as carbon dioxide.

In addition to surface processes, carbon also participates in a slow geological cycle. Carbon-containing sediments and minerals are carried deep into the Earth as tectonic plates move beneath one another, a process known as subduction (Chapter 9 has a detailed description of plate tectonics). Some of this carbon is held in the deep Earth for millions of years, while some is returned to the surface through volcanic activity and released as carbon dioxide. Together, these processes form a deep carbon cycle that helps regulate the long-term balance of carbon between Earth's interior, surface, and atmosphere. Much of this picture has emerged from recent work by the Deep Carbon Observatory, an international effort to understand carbon's behavior inside the Earth.[127]

Whether through respiration, combustion, or other means, carbon travels in cycles, from the atmosphere to the Earth, from plants to animals, but it is conserved. One may therefore reasonably wonder why there could possibly be any concern about a net increase of CO_2 in the atmosphere. The answer is that processes such as the burning of fossil fuels suddenly release large amounts of carbon dioxide from ancient carbon deposits that have been accumulating inside the Earth for eons. A large release of carbon over the blink of an eye (by geological standards) could indeed have drastic consequences on the climate. But since the carbon cycle is a dynamical system,* its behavior can be difficult to predict with confidence and is the subject of intense study (Chapter 2 has more on dynamical systems).[128] The scientific questions around this topic are quite complicated and are therefore beyond the scope of this book.

Although the carbon cycle as a whole is complex and dynamic, some of its components exhibit a remarkable regularity. In one of

* Increased atmospheric carbon creates more products for photosynthesis and can cause increased plant and microbial growth, which in turn would serve to reduce the amount of carbon in the atmosphere, and so on.

the most elegant applications of modern science, this regularity allows carbon – an element forged in stars and cycled through living organisms – to serve as a reliable measure of time.

Carbon Dating

Radiocarbon dating, commonly known as *carbon dating,* is one of the most powerful scientific tools developed in the twentieth century. The technique was developed by scientists who recognized how the mechanics of the carbon cycle could be leveraged to determine the age of organic materials.

Carbon dating relies on understanding subtle differences among carbon atoms. Although most carbon in the atmosphere is the isotope carbon-12, the textbook configuration of six protons and six neutrons, other isotopes of carbon are formed in the atmosphere. A little more than one percent of atmospheric carbon is carbon-13, which has one extra neutron, and about one in a trillion carbon atoms is carbon-14, which has two extra neutrons. Carbon-14 is continuously formed in the upper atmosphere when cosmic rays interact with nitrogen and dislodge one of its protons. As shown in Table 8.4, unlike carbon-12 and carbon-13, carbon-14 is radioactive and undergoes slow decay into nitrogen with a half-life of approximately 5,730 years.*

Chemically, however, carbon-14 behaves the same as other carbon isotopes. It is introduced into the carbon cycle as CO_2 and is distributed throughout the atmosphere, into the oceans, and to living organisms. And like all carbon, carbon-14 is similarly absorbed into living organisms through photosynthesis and metabolism, in approximately the same proportions as found in the atmosphere.

* In other words, after approximately 5,730 years, a carbon-14 atom has about a 50% chance of remaining as it is and about a 50% chance of decaying into nitrogen.

Table 8.4 Properties of naturally occurring carbon isotopes. Note that Z is the number of protons (always six for carbon), and N is the number of neutrons.

Isotope	Z	N	**Relative amount**	**Half-life**
carbon-12	6	6	~98.9%	stable
carbon-13	6	7	~1.1%	stable
carbon-14	6	8	~1 part/trillion	~5,730 yrs

Once an organism dies, it stops participating in the carbon cycle and can no longer incorporate new carbon into its structure. Then, over time, while its carbon-12 and carbon-13 isotopes remain stable, its carbon-14 isotopes decay. In 1946, University of Chicago chemist Willard Libby had the key insight that one could measure the amount of carbon-14 it contains.[129] The idea is that because carbon-14 decays at a predictable rate, its prevalence compared to other carbon isotopes would correspond to the date of the material. By 1949, Libby, together with James Arnold, had developed the instrumentation to make this theoretical idea a reality.[130]

Carbon dating has become an important tool across many fields, from archaeology, where it continues to be used to date ancient civilizations, to paleontology, where it established the ages of relatively recent organic remains. From its birth in dying stars, through cycles that connect all life on Earth, to its power to measure time itself, carbon's story spans scales from the astronomical to the atomic.

Further Explorations

Historical Notes

At the beginning of the seventeenth century, Jan Baptist van Helmont observed that when charcoal is burned, the mass of the remaining ash is notably smaller. He conjectured that something invisible – and different from ordinary air – which he termed "gas sylvestre," must have been released. By the middle of the eighteenth century, Joseph Black isolated this gas and showed it to be different from normal air. This gas is of course now known to be CO_2.

In the late eighteenth century, Joseph Priestley and Jan Ingenhousz began to understand that plants and animals participate in an exchange of gases. Priestley discovered that plants can "restore" air that had been depleted by combustion, and Ingenhousz later showed that this process requires light and produces oxygen. Both were key steps toward understanding photosynthesis.

Soon afterwards, Antoine Lavoisier conducted systematic experiments that established that combustion and respiration both consume oxygen and produce carbon dioxide, providing the foundational understanding that these processes are chemically related. These processes, including the interaction with gases in the atmosphere, became better understood in the nineteenth century by Nicolas-Théodore de Saussure, Justus von Liebig, and others.

Of course, it was not until the twentieth century that a better understanding of atomic theory and the advent of X-ray crystallography revealed the various bonding properties of carbon and its allotropes such as diamond and graphite. Atomic theory was also instrumental in Libby's development of a specialized detector for the extremely weak radioactivity emanating from carbon-14, for which he later won the Nobel Prize in chemistry.

Fred Hoyle is now credited with the theory of stellar nucleosynthesis, which explains how carbon atoms are made.* After their creation in stars, carbon atoms enter a sequence of interconnected cycles on Earth. More contemporary research on the carbon cycle

* In what many now consider a major oversight, Hoyle never won the Nobel Prize for this breakthrough work.

seeks to understand the dynamics of these cycles and their impact on the global climate.

For the Mathematically Inclined

Below are simplified chemical equations for some of the processes described in this chapter. Chemical equations can help summarize the inputs or reactants and the outputs or products of a chemical process. The reactants are shown on the left side of the arrow, and the products are shown on the right side. The substances are represented by chemical formulas, and their numerical coefficients indicate the relative amounts of the corresponding substances involved in the reaction; checking that all the atoms in a reaction are accounted for can be an instructive exercise.

The chemical equation that summarizes the inputs and outputs of photosynthesis is:

$$6CO_2 + 6H_2O + 48h\nu^* \rightarrow C_6H_{12}O_6 + 6O_2,$$
$$\text{(carbon dioxide)} + \text{(water)} + \text{(sunlight)} \rightarrow \text{(sugar/carbs)} + \text{(oxygen)}.$$

In other words, six molecules of carbon dioxide, six molecules of water, and light energy produce a molecule of glucose and six molecules of oxygen. The light energy is required because photosynthesis is an *endothermic* reaction (using energy). To produce and store the sugars and other carbohydrates, an energy input – in this case sunlight – is required.

There is also a chemical equation summarizing respiration:

$$C_6H_{12}O_6 + 6O_2 \rightarrow 6CO_2 + 6H_2O + \text{ATP},$$
$$\text{(sugar/carbs)} + \text{(oxygen)} \rightarrow \text{(carbon dioxide)} + \text{(water)} + \text{(energy)}.$$

* $h\nu$ represents the energy of a photon, where h is Planck's constant and ν is the photon's frequency. The appearance of the number 48 reflects the multi-step nature of photosynthesis: Under idealized conditions, fixing one carbon atom requires roughly 8 photons, and the formation of a glucose molecule involves 6 carbon atoms, giving a total of about 48 photons.

Respiration is an *exothermic* reaction that releases the energy from the sugars to power the cells. It produces adenosine triphosphate (ATP), which is often called the "energy currency" of cells.

Finally, when wood is burned, its cellulose and the oxygen in the air go through the following exothermic reaction:

$$C_6H_{10}O_5 + 6O_2 \rightarrow 6CO_2 + 5H_2O + \Delta H,$$
$$\text{(cellulose)} + \text{(oxygen)} \rightarrow \text{(carbon dioxide)} + \text{(water)} + \text{(heat)}.$$

It is worth noting that the plant's body is primarily composed of polymers such as cellulose, hemicellulose, and lignin. Complex processes inside the plant convert the sugars resulting from photosynthesis into these compounds roughly via the reaction: $C_6H_{12}O_6 \rightarrow C_6H_{10}O_5 + H_2O$.

Additional Reading

Carbon: One Atom's Odyssey[131] by illustrator John Barnett is a beautiful book that traces the history of a single carbon atom from its creation to the present day. This book expands on the last chapter of Primo Levi's extraordinary work, *The Periodic Table.*[132] A comprehensive book about the carbon cycle itself with a focus on flora is *The Emerald Planet: How Plants Changed Earth's History*[133] by biologist and ecologist David Beerling.

9

Shifting Ground
Plate Tectonics

Beneath the Earth's surface lie colossal slabs of rock, drifting slowly atop the planet's scorching interior. These massive plates build mountains, spread the seafloor, and set entire continents adrift. Although Earth's crust may seem solid and unyielding, it is thin and fragile compared to the fiery furnace beneath it. Modern insights into plate tectonics reveal a restless planet whose surface remains in continual motion, reshaping and renewing itself over millions of years.

But this ceaseless motion did not appear suddenly. The slow drift of continents, the rise of mountains, and the opening of ocean basins are all powered by heat left over from the planet's birth. To understand why the surface of the Earth remains in motion today, one needs to return to its formation.

Ball of Fire

About four and a half billion years ago, the Earth was nothing more than cosmic dust and debris swirling within the early solar system. Gravity slowly drew these particles together, and as they collided, their kinetic energy was converted into heat. The interior of this mass was compressed under its own weight, and the result was a molten ball of fire. Then, over hundreds of millions of years, this infernal world began its long journey toward becoming the planet it is today. The Earth's surface gradually cooled as it radiated heat into the cold vacuum of space, forming a thin, solid *crust*. Yet beneath this relatively cool exterior, the planet's heart remained a blazing furnace. Today, even after billions of years of cooling, temperatures in the Earth's core still exceed 5,000 degrees Celsius – roughly as hot as the surface of the Sun. How scientists came to know that the Earth is billions of years old, however, is a story in its own right.

Behind the modern understanding of the Earth's age is a fascinating detective story. In the late nineteenth century, the physicist Lord Kelvin calculated that the Earth could be no more than 100 million years old, based on how long a molten ball of Earth's size would take to cool to its present state.[134] His calculations were convincing, but they conflicted with geological and biological evidence – including erosion rates and the fossil record – that pointed to a much older planet. The resolution came with the discovery of radioactivity in the early twentieth century. Radioactive elements are atoms with unstable nuclei that spontaneously decay into more stable forms, releasing energy in the process. Scientists realized that billions of tons of such radioactive elements within the Earth continuously generate heat, slowing the cooling process and extending the planet's estimated lifetime by billions of years.* By the 1950s,

* Billions of tons may seem substantial, but radioactive elements comprise about 0.01% of the Earth's total mass. It may seem surprising that these are enough to so

lead isotopic dating (a technique based on the radioactive-decay ideas described in Chapter 8) produced the 4.5-billion-year figure, which agreed with both the modern understanding of physics and geological observations.

Despite its immense age and the billions of years of cooling, the Earth's solid crust remains astonishingly thin. If the Earth were scaled down to the size of an apple, its crust would be even thinner than the apple's skin. On average, the continental crust extends only about 35 kilometers deep, while the oceanic crust is even thinner at roughly seven kilometers, a mere film on the surface of a planet with a radius of over 6,300 kilometers. This fragile shell, representing about half a percent of the distance to the Earth's center, is all that separates the familiar world of mountains, oceans, and continents from the seething realm below.

The Earth's interior consists of distinct and well-defined layers, as shown in Figure 9.1. Beneath the thin, solid crust lies the *mantle*, a thick layer of hot rock that behaves as a solid on short timescales but flows slowly over millions of years. Below the mantle sits the *outer core*, composed primarily of liquid iron and nickel that generates the Earth's magnetic field through its constant motion. At the very center lies the *inner core*, where pressures are so extreme that the iron-nickel alloy is compressed back into a solid state despite temperatures rivaling those at the Sun's surface.

Moving Plates

The Earth's thin crust is bonded to the rigid uppermost portion of the mantle. Together, the crust and this upper mantle region form what geologists call the lithosphere, creating slabs typically 100 to 200 kilometers thick that are fractured into enormous *tectonic*

drastically extend the Earth's cooling time, but calculations show that it is indeed the case.

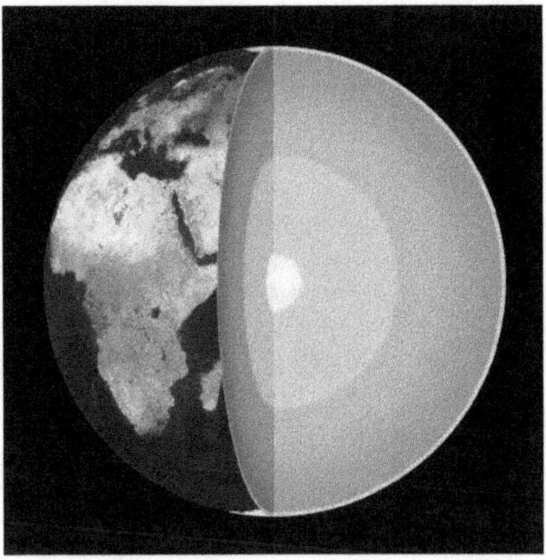

Figure 9.1 The layers on a cross-section diagram of the Earth, to scale. The crust, on the outside, is about half a percent of the Earth's radius in thickness. The next layer inward is the mantle, which goes from rigid to soft, followed by the outer core, and then the inner core at the center.[135]

plates, though compared to the radius of the Earth, these plates are still exceedingly thin. These plates creep across the mantle's asthenosphere, a more pliable zone whose elevated temperatures allow otherwise solid rock to flow.

The recognition that Earth's surface operates through a system of moving lithospheric plates that carry continents and ocean floors across the globe represented a revolutionary advance in scientific understanding. Previously, continents were thought to be permanent and immovable. In 1912, German meteorologist Alfred Wegener proposed the theory of *continental drift,* suggesting that continents had once been joined and had since moved apart.[137] As evidence, Wegener pointed to identical fossils found on opposite sides of the Atlantic Ocean, matching rock formations across continents, and ancient glacial deposits in regions that are now tropical. He hypothesized that continents had split apart from

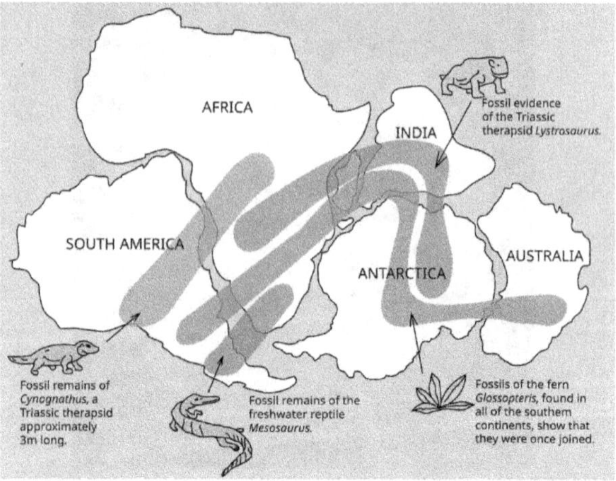

Figure 9.2 A map depicting the fossil evidence used by Wegener to support his theory of continental drift. He called this supercontinent Pangea.[136]

a primordial supercontinent he named Pangea (illustrated in Figure 9.2).* His theory was initially dismissed, and it only gained acceptance in the 1960s, when oceanographers observed seafloor spreading at mid-ocean ridges – long underwater mountain chains – and geophysicists showed that continents had moved relative to Earth's magnetic poles.[138,139]

Over time, plate tectonics has become increasingly precise and data-driven. Geologists have mapped Earth's lithosphere into 16 major tectonic plates, from the massive Pacific Plate that underlies much of the world's largest ocean to smaller but geologically active plates like the Juan de Fuca Plate off North America's west coast. These are depicted in Figure 9.3. Using satellite data, scientists can now measure plate motion with millimeter precision, confirming

* Pangea was not Earth's only supercontinent. Over the past eons, earlier supercontinents like Rodinia and Gondwana have formed and broken apart in a repeating cycle.

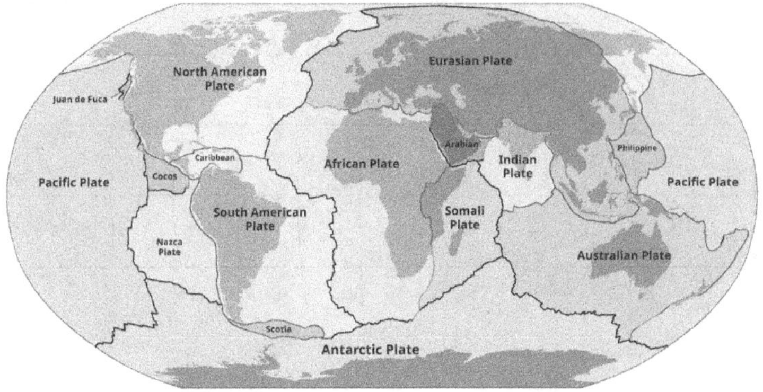

Figure 9.3 A map of Earth's 16 principal tectonic plates.[140]

that plates typically move two to ten centimeters per year. Computer models can reconstruct the positions of continents hundreds of millions of years into the past and explore their possible future configurations, indicating long-term trends such as the widening of the Atlantic Ocean and the gradual shrinking of the Pacific.

Mountains and Islands

The existence of tectonic plates not only explains otherwise mysterious fossil and geological evidence; it also beautifully accounts for geological features across the Earth. Where plates collide, mountain ranges thrust upward as continental crust crumples under immense tectonic forces. Where plates move apart, molten rock surges upward from the mantle, creating new oceanic crust and volcanic formations. Where plates slide against each other, the grinding friction generates earthquakes, the largest of which can be felt hundreds of miles from their epicenters.

Among the most striking of these geological phenomena is the Ring of Fire, a horseshoe-shaped belt of earthquake zones and

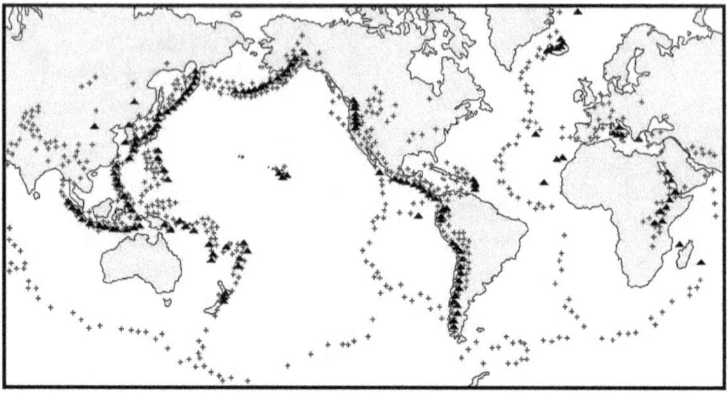

Figure 9.4 A map of the locations of earthquakes and volcanoes. The "ring" surrounding the Pacific Plate is in the center of the image.[141]

volcanoes surrounding the Pacific Plate, the largest among the 16 principal tectonic plates. As depicted in Figure 9.4, the Ring of Fire is responsible for over 90% of the world's large earthquakes and contains over 75% of the world's volcanoes. This concentration of activity results from the Pacific Plate's interactions with surrounding plates – subducting beneath some and grinding against or pulling apart from others.

Another example of tectonics producing astonishing geological formations is the Main Himalayan Thrust, the largest continental megathrust fault in the world, where the Indian and Eurasian plates converge on land in Nepal and Tibet. The continued collision of these two plates builds stresses that cause extreme earthquakes, crumpling Earth's crust and thrusting it skyward. This process has resulted in the Himalayan mountain range, which contains the tallest mountains on Earth, including Mount Everest.

Yet not all spectacular geological formations occur where plates meet. For instance, the Hawaiian Islands (shown in Figure 9.5) lie

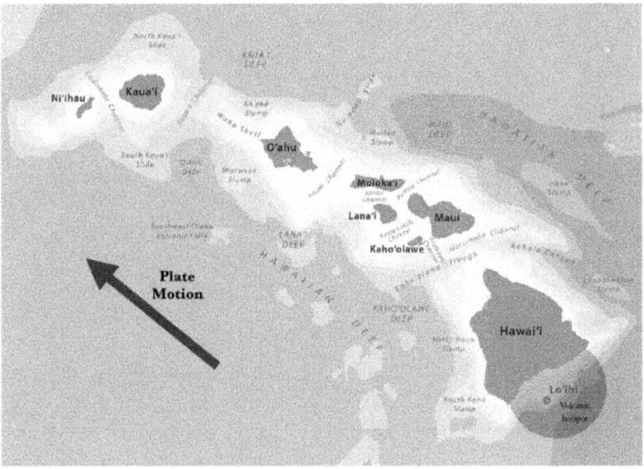

Figure 9.5 A map of the Hawaiian Islands.[142]

in the middle of the Pacific Plate, far from any plate boundary. This island chain lies above a relatively fixed "hot spot," a region where unusually hot mantle rock partially melts, producing magma that rises through the crust. When this magma reaches the surface, it erupts as lava, building volcanoes on the ocean floor. In the case of the Hawaiian archipelago, as the Pacific Plate drifts northwest, magma repeatedly reaches the surface at the hot spot, constructing large volcanic edifices that can grow high enough to emerge above sea level and form islands. The youngest island, Hawai'i (also known as The Big Island), sits at the southeastern end of the chain and is the most geologically active. Farther to the northwest lie older islands, formed when they once sat above the hot spot but were later carried away by the moving plate; over time, these older islands are worn down by erosion and gradually subside back into the Pacific.*

* In fact, stretching from Hawai'i to Russia's Kamchatka Peninsula are the Emperor Seamounts. This undersea mountain range is a series of inactive underwater volcanoes that were islands long ago when they lay above the hot spot.

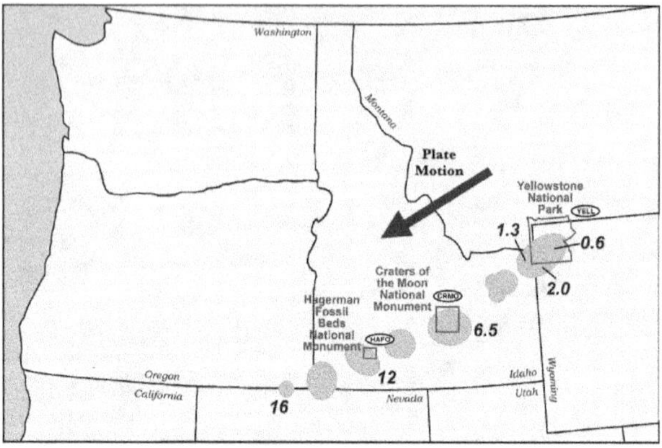

Figure 9.6 A map of the Snake River Plain. The numbers indicate, in millions of years ago, when volcanic activity is thought to have begun at those locations.[143]

When a hot spot lies under continental crust, other natural wonders can form. Yellowstone National Park also sits above a hot spot. There, heat from a vast magma chamber just beneath the surface produces astonishing geothermal features: geysers, hot springs, and mud pots. Old Faithful, the park's most famous geyser, erupts so regularly and spectacularly that it attracts millions of visitors each year. But unlike Hawai'i's steadily erupting volcanoes, Yellowstone produces rare but violent supereruptions every several hundred thousand years – the last, 640,000 years ago,* ejected enough ash to blanket much of North America, as evidenced by widespread, chemically identifiable ash layers preserved in soils and sediments across the continent. And similar to the Hawaiian island chain, the southwestward movement of the North American Plate has left behind a chain of geological wonders along the broad, low valley of the Snake River Plain. As Figure 9.6 depicts, these include

* By that rough average, another supereruption could occur soon (on Earth's timescales).

Idaho's Craters of the Moon and Hagerman Fossil Beds National Monuments.

An Ever-changing Planet

From studying plate tectonics, one thing scientists are sure about is that the Earth is anything but still. Its crust is created, reshaped, and destroyed in a slow but continual cycle. Mountains rise and crumble, islands are formed and sink, and the very ground on which billions of people live is destined eventually to be recycled into the fiery interior from which it came.

On the scale of a human lifetime, these changes are imperceptible because continents typically shift only a few centimeters per year. But if the same natural processes persist over the coming eons, the continents of the future will look very different from those of today. While scientists know the shape of continents in the past, no reliable predictions exist for the distant future. The equations governing mantle convection, which drives plate tectonics, give rise to chaotic behavior (chaos is covered in Chapter 2) over extremely large timescales.* Two hundred million years ago, the lands that New York and Morocco occupy lay side by side along the same coastline; in the far future, coastlines across the globe may be equally unrecognizable.

What is visible today is only a single frame from the Earth's ongoing transformation. Forces from deep within the Earth and from the plates themselves continually shift the positions of continents and oceans, each change building on those before it and extending into an unknown future. The boundaries between the lands and seas yet to come cannot be predicted, but as long as the planet

* Plate motion can be predicted for millions of years, but not hundreds of millions.

remains geologically active, the processes of formation and renewal will persist.

Further Explorations

Historical Notes

The idea that continents might once have been joined dates back at least to the Dutch cartographer Abraham Ortelius, who in 1596 observed that the coasts of the Americas and the combined landmasses of Europe and Africa appeared to "fit" together. He suggested that the Americas were "torn away from Europe and Africa ... The vestiges of the rupture reveal themselves, if someone brings forward a map of the world and considers carefully the coasts of the three."[144] This observation was echoed in 1858 by Antonio Snider-Pellegrini, who illustrated matching coastlines and similar fossil evidence across oceans.

In 1912, Alfred Wegener formalized the theory of continental drift, assembling compelling fossil, geological, and paleoclimate evidence. For this reason, he is regarded as the father of that theory. Yet he still lacked a convincing mechanism for moving continents. In the 1920s, British geologist Arthur Holmes proposed such a mechanism: that heat-driven convection currents in the mantle could slowly shift the continents. That idea was ahead of its time and mostly ignored until much later.

In the late 1940s, Nobel Prize-winning physicist Patrick Blackett developed highly sensitive magnetometers. These instruments enabled detailed studies of fossil magnetism in rocks, revealing patterns in Earth's magnetic field over time. Building on this capability, in 1963 geologists Fred Vine and Drummond Matthews used marine magnetometer surveys to identify symmetrical magnetic "stripes" on either side of mid-ocean ridges – clear evidence of new crust forming and moving outward. Around the same time, geologists

Harry Hess and Robert Dietz advanced the concept of seafloor spreading, showing that molten rock rises at ridges to create new oceanic crust, which then drifts away.

By the late 1960s, the combination of paleomagnetic proof, oceanographic mapping, and seafloor geology had convinced most scientists that Earth's surface is composed of moving plates. This unifying framework is known as plate tectonics.

For the Mathematically Inclined

This section will show how small rates build up to large changes over millions of years. The first example will be the Mid-Atlantic Ridge, which separates the Americas from Europe and Africa. In particular, in the North Atlantic, it separates the North American Plate from the Eurasian Plate and the African Plate, and in the South Atlantic, it separates the African and South American plates.

The Mid-Atlantic Ridge spreads at approximately 2.5 centimeters per year on average on each side. That means the continents on either side separate at $2.5 + 2.5 = 5$ centimeters per year, or 0.05 meters per year. Using the simple formula that distance = speed × time, one can calculate the distance traveled by the continents over a million years as:

$$\begin{aligned} 0.05 \text{ meters/year} \times 1{,}000{,}000 \text{ years} &= 50{,}000 \text{ meters} \\ &= 50 \text{ kilometers.} \end{aligned}$$

The Atlantic Ocean is roughly 5,000 kilometers wide at its widest. If continents drift apart 50 kilometers every million years, it should have been about

$$\frac{5{,}000 \text{ kilometers}}{50 \text{ kilometers/million years}} = 100 \text{ million years}$$

since Africa and South America began drifting apart. This rough calculation comes close to the geological estimates of 130–140 million years ago, when they were both part of Pangea.

For another example, one can consider the San Andreas Fault, which separates the Pacific and the North American plates and is responsible for many of the earthquakes in California. Los Angeles and San Francisco lie on opposite sides of the fault and also slide past each other at about 5 centimeters per year. If they continue at this rate, in just 10 million years, their relative positions would shift by

$$\begin{aligned} 0.05 \text{ meters/year} \times 10^7 \text{ years} &= 500{,}000 \text{ meters} \\ &= 500 \text{ kilometers,} \end{aligned}$$

which is somewhat larger than their current separation, so in 10 million years Los Angeles would be at a higher latitude than San Francisco!

Additional Reading

A compelling account of Lord Kelvin's (mis)calculation of the age of the Earth appears in Mario Livio's *Brilliant Blunders*[145] - some of his other chapters also have very nice connections to the topics of this book. *The Restless Earth*[146] by Nigel Calder is a classic work on plate tectonics from the 1970s, when the ideas were still new. It focuses both on the science and on the scientists. John McPhee's *Annals of the Former World*[147] is an acclaimed literary work about North America's geologic history, with sections on plate tectonics.

Epilogue

In writing this book, I wanted to share the wonders of modern science with a wider audience. As I finish, I cannot help but wonder what insights the twenty-first century might bring. Before looking ahead, though, it is worth reflecting on the themes that have emerged throughout this book.

The first is that our knowledge has fundamental limits. Gödel and Turing showed that there are mathematical truths we can never uncover; Heisenberg extended this principle to physics, revealing limits to what can be measured. This dovetails with Lorenz's discovery that small uncertainties can cascade into much larger ones. Whereas earlier science aspired to construct complete and rigorous systems of the world, modern science has forced us all to live with uncertainty and doubt.

The second is that complexity and unpredictability often arise from simplicity. Turing machines are minimal devices, yet they give rise to problems of staggering intricacy. Newton's three simple laws are enough to produce chaotic behavior.* Just four base pairs encode DNA, yet they encompass the vast diversity of life on Earth. An elegant theory of slowly drifting continents explains countless puzzles, including those in the fossil record.

* Newton's laws are, of course, only approximations, and they break down at extreme scales. While quantum mechanics and general relativity cannot yet give a full account of physics, most scientists believe that whatever grand unified theory eventually emerges will, in some sense, be simple and elegant.

Both these themes demand a kind of humility. We cannot know everything, and even what we can know may resist prediction. For example, after the invention of atomic weapons, many expected physics to continue its explosive pace of discovery – but it was computing, not physics, that made the largest leaps in the decades to follow. Keeping this in mind, I still want to speculate about the future. By examining how today's advances differ from those that defined the last century, we can try to guess where science may be headed next.

Already, artificial intelligence systems are beginning to make genuine discoveries – from coming up with new explanations for physical phenomena to contributing to mathematics, where general-purpose models such as `ChatGPT` are helping to prove new theorems. Many of these systems take advantage of vast amounts of data, and that data is no longer merely a tool to guide theory; it has become a source of insight in its own right, especially when coupled with neural networks that can detect patterns beyond human intuition. These technologies are already impressive, but they are only in their infancy.

I expect that such systems will continue to accelerate scientific discovery. This has tremendous promise – not only for advancing fundamental knowledge but also for improving human life and flourishing. Yet it also raises profound questions. What form will these discoveries take? As discussed in Chapter 6, `AlphaFold` predicts protein structures with remarkable accuracy, but it is harder to say that we know exactly what it is doing. I think it likely that science will move further in this direction, producing results that can be verified but not understood, at least not in the traditional sense.*

* A similar situation can arise in mathematics, where computer-checkable proofs may establish the correctness of theorems yet remain too complex for humans to grasp in their entirety.

We may well be standing at the brink of another scientific revolution, one in which human curiosity and artificial intelligence combine to produce new science in ways we are only beginning to glimpse. How long humans will remain essential to this process is itself uncertain; it is yet another of the many uncertainties we continue to face in making sense of modern science.

Acknowledgments

I first wish to express my deep gratitude to Katie Leach, my editor at Cambridge University Press. From the earliest stages of this project, she supported the book idea and guided it with insight and enthusiasm. She made every step of the process – from proposal review to development and editing – painless and even enjoyable. I am especially grateful for her many thoughtful suggestions, which greatly improved the book. I also thank Katie's editorial assistant, Arman Chowdhury, for his contributions to the editing process.

I am indebted to the book's proposal and development reviewers for helping keep the science and other information as accurate as possible. Writing a book that spans so many diverse fields means that I cannot be an expert in all of them – a fact of which I am very aware. For this reason, each chapter was reviewed by multiple experts in its field. Although anonymous, their feedback was invaluable, and I deeply appreciate the time and attention they devoted to this task.

I am also grateful to my family and friends for their many contributions. Their comments helped me clarify my thinking, correct misconceptions, understand my audience, and ultimately tell a better story. I thank: Genie Elson, Yuri Elson, Aryeh Kontorovich, Alex Reyzin, Marina Reyzin, Sofiya Reyzin, and Deepika Vasudevan. I was also fortunate to work with Olga Hautin, who created the book's beautiful cover artwork. Finally, I owe particular thanks to those closest to me for encouraging and supporting this project from its inception.

Glossary of Terms

activation function (φ): a (usually nonlinear) function applied to a neuron's weighted sum that determines the neuron's output.
aether (luminiferous aether): a hypothetical medium once proposed to fill space and carry light waves, later abandoned after experiments and relativity showed it was unnecessary.
algorithm: a precise, step-by-step procedure for solving a problem or performing a computation that transforms inputs into desired outputs.
allele: a version of a gene occupying a specific location on a chromosome.
alpha helix: a spiral structural motif in proteins formed by hydrogen bonds along the peptide backbone, giving rise to helical stability and elasticity.
allotropes: different structural forms of the same element distinguished by how atoms bond and arrange in space (e.g., diamond and graphite for carbon).
amino acid: an organic molecule that serves as a basic building block of proteins.
amplitude (quantum amplitude): a complex number whose squared magnitude gives a quantum event's probability; amplitudes can interfere constructively or destructively.
amplitude cancellation: the destructive interference of quantum amplitudes that reduces or eliminates the probability of an outcome when wave components oppose in phase.
Ampère's law: a principle of electromagnetism stating that electric currents produce magnetic fields, with the magnetic field

circulating around the current in proportion to its strength.
angular momentum: a measure of the tendency of an object to keep rotating and the direction of rotation.
architecture (neural network architecture): the design specifying how neurons and layers connect within a neural network, including depth, width, and type of layers.
artificial intelligence (AI): the field that studies methods for getting computers to make decisions or predictions, often by learning from data rather than following only hand-coded rules.
artificial neuron: a simplified mathematical model inspired by the brain's neuron; it receives weighted inputs, sums them, and applies an activation function to produce an output.
asymmetric game: a game in which players have different strategies, payoffs, or information, so their positions are not interchangeable.
asthenosphere: the semi-molten layer of the upper mantle beneath the lithosphere that allows tectonic plates to move through slow, viscous flow.
ATP (adenosine triphosphate): the molecule that stores and transfers energy within cells by releasing phosphate bonds, powering nearly all biological work.
attractor: the set a dynamical system tends to settle into over time, such as a fixed point, a repeating cycle, or a chaotic limiting pattern.
atomic number (Z): the number of protons in an atom's nucleus, which defines its chemical identity and position in the periodic table.
atomic stability: the fact that electrons occupy stable, quantized bound states around a nucleus rather than collapsing inward.
atom: the smallest unit of an element retaining its chemical identity, composed of a nucleus of protons and neutrons surrounded by electrons.
backpropagation: the learning algorithm used to adjust neural-network weights by propagating output errors backward through the layers to compute gradients efficiently.

base pairing (A–T, G–C): the specific hydrogen bonding of complementary nucleotides that underlies DNA's double-helix structure: adenine with thymine and guanine with cytosine.
Bayesian game: a strategic game in which players have incomplete information about others' types or payoffs but hold probabilistic beliefs guiding rational decisions.
beam splitter / recombiner: an optical device that divides a beam of light or particles into two paths and can later recombine them to produce interference effects.
best response: a strategy that yields the highest possible payoff for a player, given the strategies chosen by the other players.
beta sheet: a secondary protein structure formed by neighboring polypeptide strands connected through hydrogen bonds, creating a sheet-like arrangement.
bifurcation: a qualitative change in a system where, as a parameter crosses a critical value, a single stable behavior splits into two distinct branches of possible behavior.
Big Bang: the model in which the universe has been expanding from a much hotter, denser early state for about 13.8 billion years.
biochemistry: the study of the chemical processes and molecules that constitute and sustain life.
black hole: a region where gravity is strong enough that light cannot escape, often formed from collapsed massive stars.
blending theory: an outdated pre-Mendelian theory of inheritance proposing that offspring traits are averaged mixtures of their parents' traits.
bounded rationality: the concept that decision-makers aim for satisfactory rather than optimal choices due to limited information, computation, or time.
Boveri–Sutton theory (chromosomal theory of inheritance): the early-twentieth-century realization that genes reside on chromosomes, which segregate and assort during reproduction to transmit heredity.

Brouwer's fixed point theorem: a mathematical statement that any continuous function mapping a compact convex set to itself has at least one fixed point.
butterfly effect: the sensitivity of chaotic systems to initial conditions, where tiny differences can grow exponentially and lead to vastly different outcomes.
calculus: the branch of mathematics dealing with continuous change through differentiation and integration, providing the language of motion and forces.
Calvin cycle: the sequence of enzyme-driven reactions in photosynthesis that converts CO_2 into sugars using energy from ATP and NADPH.
carbon cycle: the continual movement of carbon among the atmosphere, oceans, rocks, and living organisms through processes like photosynthesis, respiration, and combustion.
carbon dating (radiocarbon dating): a method for determining the age of organic materials by measuring the remaining amount of radioactive carbon-14 relative to stable carbon isotopes.
central dogma of molecular biology: the principle that genetic information flows in one direction – from DNA to RNA to proteins.
chaos theory: the mathematical study of deterministic systems whose long-term behavior is unpredictable because of extreme sensitivity to initial conditions.
chaotic system: a deterministic system whose long-term behavior is unpredictable because small uncertainties in initial values grow rapidly over time.
charge density (relativistic effect): the measured concentration of electric charge in a given reference frame.
chaperone proteins: specialized proteins that assist other proteins in folding into their proper three-dimensional shapes and prevent misfolding.

chlorophyll: the green pigment in plants and algae that captures light energy for photosynthesis by absorbing mainly red and blue wavelengths.

chromosome: a long, organized strand of DNA and proteins carrying many genes, found in the cell nucleus and responsible for heredity.

Church–Turing thesis: the proposition that anything computable by any physical means can be computed by a Turing machine.

clustered regularly interspaced short palindromic repeats (CRISPR): Repetitive DNA sequences in bacteria that, with associated Cas proteins, provide adaptive immunity by cutting matching viral DNA.

codon: a triplet of RNA bases encoding a specific amino acid or a start/stop signal; redundancy in the third "wobble" position enables error tolerance.

combustion: a chemical reaction between a fuel and oxygen that releases heat and light, usually by converting stored chemical energy into CO_2 and H_2O.

Compton scattering: the effect in which a photon collides with a charged particle, losing energy and changing wavelength, providing evidence of light's particle nature.

complexity (and its emergence from simple rules): the appearance of rich, organized behavior produced by many simple interactions repeated over time.

complex number: a number of the form $a + bi$ that extends real numbers to include the imaginary unit $i = \sqrt{-1}$, used in describing wave behavior and quantum mechanics.

computational complexity: the study of how an algorithm's time, memory, or other requirements grow as the input size increases.

computational efficiency: a measure of how economically an algorithm uses resources such as time and memory.

computational thinking: a style of reasoning that formulates problems and their solutions in terms of algorithmic steps.

convection currents: the cyclical movement of fluid or mantle material driven by temperature differences, where warmer material rises and cooler material sinks.
constructive interference: the reinforcement of waves when their phases align, increasing amplitude or intensity at the meeting point.
continental drift: the gradual movement of Earth's continents across the globe due to plate tectonics.
convolutional neural network (CNN): a type of deep neural network designed to process data with a spatial or grid-like structure, using layers to extract hierarchical features from images or signals.
Cook–Levin theorem: the result showing that the Boolean satisfiability problem (SAT) is NP-complete, establishing the formal basis for the class of NP-complete problems.
cosmic rays: high-energy particles, mostly protons and atomic nuclei, originating from outer space and striking Earth's atmosphere at near-light speeds.
covalent bond: a chemical bond formed when atoms share pairs of electrons, creating stable molecules.
CRISPR-associated (Cas) proteins: enzymes that work with CRISPR sequences to identify and cut specific DNA segments, enabling precise gene editing.
CRISPR loci: specific regions in bacterial DNA containing CRISPR repeats and stored viral sequences that guide Cas proteins in future defenses.
crust: the thin, outermost layer of a planet or moon, lying above the mantle and composed of solid rock.
cryptography: the science of securing information through mathematical transformations that enable encryption, authentication, and privacy.
cyanobacteria (blue-green algae): photosynthetic microorganisms that use sunlight to produce energy and oxygen.

cyclic compound: a molecule in which atoms are connected in a closed ring, often contributing to stability and chemical reactivity, as in benzene.

deep learning: a machine learning technique that uses multi-layered neural networks that automatically learn representations through successive transformations of the data.

denaturation: the loss of a protein's or nucleic acid's structure and function due to heat, chemicals, or pH changes, without breaking its primary bonds.

detector (quantum measurement device): an instrument that interacts with quantum particles to register measurable outcomes, collapsing superpositions into definite states.

Deutsch's problem: a theoretical task demonstrating how a quantum computer can determine whether a function is constant or balanced using only one evaluation, a speedup over a classical computer.

deoxyribonucleic acid (DNA): the molecule carrying genetic information in all living organisms, composed of nucleotide sequences arranged in a double helix.

destructive interference: the cancellation of overlapping waves whose phases are opposite, reducing or eliminating total amplitude.

deterministic game: a game in which outcomes follow directly from players' actions, with no randomness or chance influencing results.

deterministic unpredictability: behavior that follows exact rules but is in practice hard to forecast because of sensitivity to initial conditions.

diagonalization (Cantor's argument): a mathematical technique showing that some sets (like real numbers) are uncountably infinite.

Diffie–Hellman key exchange: a cryptographic protocol that allows two parties to establish a shared secret over an insecure channel.

diffraction: the spreading or bending of waves as they pass around an obstacle or through a narrow opening.

Dirac notation (bra-ket notation): a compact formalism in quantum mechanics that represents quantum states as "kets" $|\psi\rangle$ (and their duals as "bras" $\langle\psi|$).

discrete dynamical system: a system whose state evolves in discrete time steps according to a specific rule, often exhibiting periodic or chaotic patterns.

discrete logarithm: the inverse of modular exponentiation, difficult to compute efficiently, forming the basis of many cryptographic systems.

discrete logarithm problem: the computational problem of finding exponents in modular arithmetic, which is believed to be hard and used for cryptographic security.

dissipative system: a physical system in which energy is lost over time, typically as heat, so that motion or activity gradually diminishes unless energy is supplied from outside.

double helix: the twisted-ladder structure of DNA, where two strands wind around each other and are held together by base pairings.

double-slit experiment: a key demonstration of quantum interference showing that particles like photons and electrons can behave as waves and self-interfere.

drift velocity: the average velocity of charged particles, such as electrons, as they move through a conductor under an electric field.

duopoly (Cournot model): a market structure with two competing producers whose output decisions jointly determine the market price and equilibrium.

dynamical system: any system, physical or mathematical, that evolves in time according to specific rules (often described by differential or difference equations).

Earth's axis (tilted axis): the imaginary line about which Earth rotates, tilted about 23.5° relative to its orbital plane, producing seasonal changes.

earthquake: a sudden release of energy within Earth's crust or upper mantle, producing seismic waves that shake the ground.

electric charge (positive, negative): a fundamental property of matter causing electromagnetic interactions, with opposite charges attracting and like charges repelling.

electric force (Coulomb force): the attractive or repulsive interaction between charged particles, governed by Coulomb's inverse-square law.

electrical current: the rate of flow of electric charge through a conductor, measured in amperes.

electromagnetic force: one of the four fundamental forces of nature, combining electricity and magnetism into a single interaction between charged particles.

electromagnetic wave: a self-propagating oscillation of electric and magnetic fields that travels through space at the speed of light.

electromagnetism: the unified theory describing the relationship between electric and magnetic fields and their effects on matter and radiation.

electron: a fundamental particle with negative charge and very small mass, orbiting atomic nuclei and participating in electric and chemical processes.

endothermic reaction: a chemical reaction that absorbs heat energy from its surroundings, requiring energy input to proceed.

energetically favorable state: the configuration of a system with minimal potential energy, toward which natural processes tend to evolve.

entanglement: a quantum phenomenon in which two or more particles share a single joint state, so that measurements on one are correlated with outcomes on the others, regardless of the distance between them.

Entscheidungsproblem (decision problem): the problem of whether a general algorithm exists to decide the truth of any mathematical statement that was shown unsolvable by Alan Turing.

error correction: the detection of mistakes and the recovery of intended information using redundancy or structured encoding.

equivalence principle: the principle that gravitational acceleration is locally indistinguishable from acceleration due to motion.

evolution by natural selection: the process by which organisms with advantageous heritable traits reproduce more successfully.

evolutionarily stable strategy (ESS): in evolutionary game theory, a strategy that, once adopted by a population, cannot be invaded by alternative strategies.

exothermic reaction: a reaction that releases heat energy, typically occurring spontaneously once initiated.

explanatory framework: a connected set of concepts and principles that account for a range of observations and phenomena.

expectation (or expected value): the average outcome of a random variable, calculated by weighting each possible value by the probability that it occurs.

expected payoff: the average outcome a player can expect in a probabilistic game, computed by weighting each payoff by its probability.

expected utility: a measure of rational choice that evaluates uncertain options based on their possible outcomes weighted by subjective preferences.

exponential (in computational complexity): growing so that each constant increase in input size multiplies the amount of computation required.

ex vivo: describes biological experiments or treatments conducted on cells or tissues outside the living organism, under controlled laboratory conditions.

factorial growth: a rapid rate of increase proportional to $n!$, where quantities expand faster than exponential functions.

Faraday's law (electromagnetic induction): the principle that a changing magnetic field induces an electric current, forming the basis for generators.

fault: a fracture or boundary between tectonic plates along which movement causes earthquakes.

finite game: a game with a limited number of players, possible actions, and outcomes.

finite group: a mathematical set with a finite number of elements that satisfy closure, associativity, identity, and invertibility under a given operation.

fixed point: a value or state that remains unchanged under a given function or transformation, often representing equilibrium.

Fleming's left-hand rule: a mnemonic used to determine the direction of force on a current-carrying conductor in a magnetic field.

Fleming's right-hand rule: a rule used to find the direction of induced current when a conductor moves through a magnetic field.

food chain: the sequence of organisms through which energy and nutrients pass as one species eats another.

fractal: a self-similar geometric pattern repeating at multiple scales, often arising in nature and chaotic systems.

fullerenes: hollow, cage-like molecules made entirely of carbon atoms arranged in interconnected rings, forming closed structures with distinctive chemical and physical properties.

Galilean invariance: the principle that the fundamental laws of mechanics are the same in all inertial reference frames.

game: a formal model of strategic interaction in which multiple decision-makers choose actions, and each participant's outcome depends on the actions chosen by all players.

game theory: the mathematical study of strategic interactions among rational agents whose outcomes depend on one another's choices.

game value: the equilibrium payoff guaranteed to a player in an optimal strategy of a zero-sum game.

gene: a unit of heredity encoded in DNA that determines specific traits by directing protein synthesis.

gene editing: the deliberate alteration of DNA sequences in an organism, typically using technologies like CRISPR–Cas.

gene expression: the process by which genetic information is transcribed and translated into functional proteins or RNA molecules.

genetics: the study of genes, inheritance, and the variation of traits in living organisms.

general relativity: Einstein's theory describing gravity as the curvature of spacetime caused by mass and energy.

general-sum game: a game in which players' payoffs need not add to zero, allowing for cooperation or mutual benefit.

geological time: the immense timescale over which Earth's physical and biological processes occur, measured in millions or billions of years.

germ theory of disease: the explanation that microorganisms cause infectious diseases, replacing earlier "miasma" theories.

Gödel's incompleteness theorem: the proof that any sufficiently complex formal system contains true statements that cannot be proven within the system.

graphics processing unit (GPU): a processor optimized for parallel computation, originally for graphics but now essential in deep learning.

gravity as spacetime curvature: the general relativistic view that mass and energy curve spacetime, producing what is perceived as gravitational attraction.

gravitational lensing: the deflection of light by massive objects, confirming general relativity and enabling cosmic observations.

half-life: the time required for half the atoms of a radioactive substance to decay into another element or isotope.

halting problem: the undecidable problem of whether a computer program will eventually stop running or loop forever.

heliocentric model: the astronomical model placing the Sun at the center of the solar system with planets orbiting around it.

Hilbert space (state vector space): a complete mathematical space used in quantum mechanics to represent all possible states of a system.

Homo sapiens: the modern human species, characterized by advanced cognition, language, and culture.

hot spot: a stationary area in Earth's mantle where heat rises and melts the crust above, forming volcano chains like the Hawaiian Islands.

hybridization (of orbitals): the mixing of atomic orbitals into new shapes that explain the bonding geometries of molecules.

imperfect information game: a game in which players lack full knowledge of others' actions or payoffs, as in poker.

in vivo: describes biological experiments or treatments performed directly within a living organism rather than in isolated cells.

inertial reference frame: a coordinate system in which objects in motion remain in uniform motion unless acted upon by a force (i.e., where Newton's first law holds).

information theory: the mathematical study of information, measuring how data can be represented and transmitted efficiently and reliably, often using redundancy to correct errors.

inner core: the solid, dense center of Earth composed mainly of iron and nickel, where extreme pressure keeps it solid despite high temperatures.

interference pattern: the pattern of alternating intensities formed when waves overlap, showing areas of constructive and destructive interference.

interferometer: a device that splits and recombines waves, such as light or particles, to measure interference and detect small differences in distance or phase.

isotope: a variant of a chemical element that has the same number of protons but different numbers of neutrons, often used for dating and tracing.

Kepler's laws: three empirical laws describing how planets orbit the Sun in ellipses, sweep equal areas in equal times, and have orbital periods related to their distances.
kinetic energy: the energy an object possesses due to its motion, proportional to its mass and the square of its velocity.
label (classification label): the category or class assigned to an input in supervised machine learning, representing the correct output during training.
large language model (LLM): a neural network trained on vast amounts of text to predict and generate language.
lead isotopic dating: a radiometric dating method that measures ratios of lead isotopes to determine the age of rocks or meteorites.
LED (light-emitting diode): a semiconductor device that emits light when an electric current passes through it, used for efficient illumination and displays.
length contraction (Lorentz contraction): the relativistic shortening of an object's length along its direction of motion, observed when moving at speeds close to the speed of light.
ligase: an enzyme that joins two DNA or RNA fragments together.
limit cycle: a closed trajectory in the state space of a dynamical system that represents periodic, self-sustaining oscillations.
lithosphere: the Earth's rigid outer layer that is made up of the crust and the uppermost mantle and divided into tectonic plates.
logistic map: a simple recursive equation $x_{n+1} = rx_n(1 - x_n)$ that demonstrates how deterministic systems can exhibit chaos.
Lorentz factor: the scaling factor in special relativity that determines time dilation and length contraction.
Lorenz attractor: the butterfly-shaped trajectory formed by solutions of the Lorenz equations, illustrating deterministic chaos.
Lorenz system: a set of nonlinear differential equations modeling atmospheric convection, known for producing chaotic behavior.
lunar eclipse: the alignment when Earth passes between the Sun and Moon, casting its shadow on the lunar surface.

machine learning: the field of computer science focused on algorithms that learn patterns from data and improve their performance without explicit programming.
magnetic field: the region around a magnet or moving electric charge where magnetic forces can be observed.
magnetic force: the force exerted on a moving charge or magnetic material in the presence of a magnetic field.
magnetic pole (north/south polarity): the two regions of a magnet where magnetic field lines converge (south) or diverge (north).
magnetism as a relativistic effect: the phenomenon that magnetism arises as a consequence of relativity, due to moving electric charges and length contraction.
mantle: the thick layer of semi-solid rock between Earth's crust and core that slowly flows and drives plate motion.
mantle convection: the slow circulation of material in Earth's mantle caused by temperature differences, powering plate tectonics.
messenger RNA (mRNA): the RNA molecule that carries genetic instructions from DNA to ribosomes for protein synthesis.
metabolism: the chemical reactions in living organisms that convert energy and materials to sustain life.
mid-ocean ridge: a continuous underwater mountain chain formed by seafloor spreading where tectonic plates diverge.
minimax theorem: von Neumann's result stating that in zero-sum games, each player has an optimal strategy minimizing his maximum possible expected loss.
modulo operation (mod): a mathematical operation that returns the remainder after dividing one number by another.
multi-player game: a strategic interaction involving more than two participants.
muon: a heavier cousin of the electron, unstable and decaying into lighter particles with a mean lifetime of about 2 microseconds.

muon decay (half-life): the radioactive-like process by which muons spontaneously transform into electrons and neutrinos, with a characteristic half-life.

mutation (silent mutation): a change in the genetic code that may or may not alter protein structure; a silent mutation changes DNA but not the amino acid sequence.

MRI (magnetic resonance imaging): a medical imaging technique using magnetic fields and radio waves to generate detailed internal body images.

Nash equilibrium: a stable outcome in which no player can benefit by unilaterally changing his strategy, given the strategies of others.

Navier–Stokes equations: the differential equations governing the motion of viscous fluids, fundamental to fluid dynamics.

nearest-neighbor algorithm: a simple machine learning method that classifies points by the most common label among their closest training examples.

neural network: a system of interconnected artificial neurons that learns to approximate complex functions through weight adjustment.

neutron: an electrically neutral particle in the atomic nucleus with a mass slightly greater than that of the proton.

neutron star: the dense stellar remnant left after a supernova, composed almost entirely of neutrons and possessing intense gravity.

Newton's laws of motion: three principles established by Isaac Newton describing the relationship between forces and the motion of objects.

nitrogen base (adenine [A], cytosine [C], guanine [G], thymine [T]): the four molecular units that form the rungs of the DNA ladder and encode genetic information.

non-cooperative game: a game in which players make independent decisions without enforceable agreements or alliances.

nonlinear ordinary differential equation (ODE): a differential equation in which the unknown function or its derivatives appear with powers or products, often producing complex behavior.
nonlinear system: a system whose output is not directly proportional to its input, allowing for feedback, bifurcations, and chaos.
normalization: the process of scaling a vector so that its magnitude equals one, often used to represent probability amplitudes.
NP: the class of computational problems whose proposed solutions can be verified efficiently (these problems are not necessarily efficiently solvable).
NP-completeness: a property of certain computational problems that are both in NP and as hard as any problem in NP, meaning a fast solution to one would yield fast solutions to all NP problems.
nucleotide: the molecular building block of nucleic acids, consisting of a sugar, phosphate group, and nitrogen base.
nuclear brinkmanship: the strategic use of threats involving nuclear weapons to gain advantage in political or military negotiations.
nuclear fusion: the process in which atomic nuclei combine to form heavier elements, releasing large amounts of energy.
observable: a measurable physical property in quantum mechanics, represented mathematically by an operator acting on a state.
one-way function: a function that is easy to compute in one direction but hard to invert, fundamental to modern cryptography.
orbit (Earth's revolution around the Sun): the curved path of Earth or any celestial body as it travels under the influence of gravity.
orbital motion: the regular trajectory of an object around another due to gravitational or electromagnetic attraction.
organic chemistry: the branch of chemistry that studies carbon-based compounds, including their structures, reactions, and properties.
outer core: the liquid layer of molten metal surrounding Earth's inner core, whose movement generates the planet's magnetic field.

P: the class of computational problems solvable efficiently in polynomial time.
P vs. NP problem: the central question of whether every problem whose solution can be verified quickly can also be solved quickly.
payoff: the numerical value representing the outcome or utility a player receives from a specific strategy in a game.
payoff matrix: a table listing players' possible strategies and the corresponding outcomes or utilities for each combination.
Peano axioms: a set of rules defining the natural numbers and basic arithmetic operations.
periodic table (classification of elements): a systematic arrangement of elements by atomic number and chemical properties.
perfect information game: a game in which all players know the full history of moves and available strategies, such as chess.
perceptron: a simple type of artificial neuron that linearly combines inputs and applies a threshold-based activation to produce an output.
phase difference: the relative position of two oscillations within their cycles at a given moment, indicating how much one wave leads or lags another in time or space.
photon: the smallest unit of light, carrying energy proportional to its frequency and mediating electromagnetic interactions.
photoelectric effect: the emission of electrons from a material when struck by light, demonstrating that light has particle-like properties.
photosynthesis: the process by which plants and some microorganisms convert sunlight, water, and carbon dioxide into sugars and oxygen.
Planck constant (h): the proportionality constant linking a photon's energy to its frequency, central to quantum mechanics.
planetary orbits: the elliptical paths of planets around the Sun as described by Kepler's laws and Newtonian gravity.
player: an agent or decision-maker in a game who selects strategies to maximize payoffs.

plate tectonics: the theory explaining Earth's lithosphere as divided into moving plates whose interactions form mountains, volcanoes, and earthquakes.
polarization: the property of a wave that specifies the orientation of its oscillations, describing how the wave vibrates in directions perpendicular to its propagation.
polymer: a large molecule composed of repeating subunits; in plants, polymers form structural materials like cellulose and lignin.
polypeptide: a linear chain of amino acids that folds into a specific shape to form a protein.
polynomial time (the class P): describes algorithms whose running time grows at most as a polynomial function of input size, considered efficient.
prime number: a natural number greater than 1 that has no positive divisors other than 1 and itself.
prisoner's dilemma: a game-theoretic scenario in which two rational players, acting in their own self-interest, choose actions that lead to a worse outcome for both than if they had cooperated.
private key / secret key: the confidential key used in cryptographic systems to decrypt or sign information.
probability amplitude (constructive/destructive interference): a complex-valued quantity in quantum mechanics whose square gives probability and whose sign allows interference.
protein: a large biological molecule made of amino acids, responsible for catalyzing reactions, signaling, and providing structure in living organisms.
protein folding: the process by which a polypeptide chain assumes its functional three-dimensional shape based on energetic stability.
protein structure (primary, secondary, tertiary, quaternary): the four hierarchical levels describing a protein's organization, from amino acid sequence to multi-subunit assembly.
proton: a positively charged subatomic particle found in the nucleus.

public key: the openly shared key in asymmetric cryptography used for encryption or signature verification.

public-key cryptography: cryptographic systems using public and private keys to allow for secure communication without shared secrets.

qubit (quantum bit): the basic unit of quantum information that can exist in a superposition of 0 and 1 states simultaneously.

quantum advantage: the performance edge that quantum computers achieve over classical ones for certain computational tasks.

quantum collapse: the sudden transition of a quantum system from a superposition of states to a definite outcome upon measurement.

quantum computer: a computational device that performs calculations using qubits and quantum operations exploiting superposition and entanglement.

quantum decoherence: the process by which quantum systems lose coherence due to interaction with their environment, appearing classical.

quantum mechanics: the theory describing the behavior of matter and energy at atomic and subatomic scales.

quantum operation: a mathematical transformation that evolves or measures quantum states.

quantum tunneling: the quantum effect where particles pass through potential barriers that would be impassable classically.

radioactive decay: the spontaneous transformation of an unstable atomic nucleus into a more stable form, releasing energy or particles in the process.

radioactivity: the property of certain elements or isotopes to emit radiation as they go through radioactive decay.

recursive system: a system whose output at each stage depends on the results of previous stages.

reduction (problem reduction): a procedure that transforms one problem into another.

refraction: the bending of light (or other waves) as it passes from one medium to another.
refractive index: a measure of how much a medium slows down light.
relativistic electrodynamics: the unified framework combining electromagnetism with special relativity, describing electric and magnetic fields consistently for moving observers.
relativistic mass–energy equivalence ($E = mc^2$): Einstein's relation stating that mass and energy are interchangeable forms of the same quantity.
relativistic speed: a velocity comparable to the speed of light, at which relativistic effects like time dilation and length contraction become significant.
repeated game (iterated game): a game-theoretic setting in which the same game is played multiple times by the same players.
replication: the biological process of copying DNA so that genetic information is transmitted during cell division.
respiration (cellular): the set of biochemical processes by which a cell breaks down nutrients to release energy, producing ATP to power cellular activities.
restriction enzyme: a bacterial enzyme that cuts DNA at specific recognition sequences, used in genetic engineering and molecular biology.
Rice's theorem: a result in computability theory stating that all nontrivial semantic properties of programs are undecidable.
ribosome: the cellular molecular machine that translates mRNA sequences into amino acid chains, producing proteins.
right-hand grip rule (Ampère's rule): a mnemonic that determines the direction of a magnetic field around a current-carrying conductor.
RNA nucleotides (adenine [A], uracil [U], guanine [G], cytosine [C]): the four chemical bases forming RNA, analogous to DNA but with uracil replacing thymine.

rule-based systems: early artificial intelligence models that apply explicit logical rules to make decisions or draw conclusions.

scientific revolution: a period of major transformation in scientific thought during which new methods, experiments, and theories emerged.

seasons (astronomical explanation): the cyclical variations in climate and daylight caused by Earth's tilted axis as it orbits the Sun.

self-similarity: the property of a structure or process in which parts resemble the whole at different scales, typical of fractals.

sensitivity to initial conditions: the defining feature of chaotic systems where small differences in starting points lead to vastly different outcomes.

shared secret: a confidential value known only to communicating parties, used in cryptographic protocols for secure communication.

simultaneity (relativity of simultaneity): the concept that whether two events occur at the same time depends on the observer's frame of reference.

simultaneous game: a game in which all players choose their actions without knowledge of the others' choices.

sorting algorithm: a computational procedure that orders elements of a list according to a defined criterion, such as numerical or lexicographic order.

spacetime: the four-dimensional continuum combining space and time into a single framework in relativity theory.

special relativity: Einstein's 1905 theory showing that the laws of physics are the same in all inertial frames and that time and space are interrelated.

spin (electron spin): the intrinsic angular momentum of quantum particles, giving rise to magnetic and quantum effects.

start codon/stop codon: triplets in mRNA that signal where translation begins and ends during protein synthesis.

stellar nucleosynthesis: the process by which stars create new atomic nuclei through nuclear fusion, forming elements heavier than hydrogen and helium.

stochastic game: a dynamic game that incorporates randomness in transitions between states.

strange attractor: a geometric structure in a chaotic system's state space that exhibits non-repeating yet bounded trajectories.

strategy (pure strategy, mixed strategy): a rule or plan dictating how a player acts in a game; pure strategies are fixed choices, mixed involve randomness.

subduction: the process by which one tectonic plate sinks beneath another into the mantle, forming trenches and volcanic arcs.

subgame-perfect equilibrium: a refinement of Nash equilibrium in sequential games requiring optimal strategies in every subgame.

supernova: a massive stellar explosion marking the death of a star, dispersing heavy elements into space.

superposition: the quantum principle that systems can exist in multiple states simultaneously until measured.

supercontinent (Pangea, Rodinia, Gondwana): a large landmass composed of multiple continents joined together, recurring throughout Earth's history.

synthetic biology: the engineering of biological systems and organisms for useful purposes by redesigning genetic material.

symmetric game: a game where the payoffs and available strategies are identical for all players.

tectonic plate: a massive slab of the lithosphere that moves over Earth's mantle, interacting with other plates at boundaries.

thermodynamics: the branch of physics studying energy, heat, and work, and the laws governing their transformation.

theory of relativity: Einstein's combined framework of special and general relativity explaining motion, gravity, and spacetime geometry.

three-body problem: the problem of predicting the motion of three gravitationally interacting bodies, which often leads to chaotic behavior.

time dilation: the slowing of time observed for an object in motion relative to a stationary observer or in a gravitational field.

time dilation equation: the formula describing how time stretches at relativistic speeds.

tipping point: a threshold at which a small change causes a sudden and sometimes irreversible shift in the behavior of a system.

training data: the dataset used to teach a machine-learning model by providing examples with known outcomes.

transcription: the process of copying DNA into messenger RNA as the first step of gene expression.

transformer: a neural-network architecture built around attention, which lets the model weigh which parts of an input sequence matter most for predicting the next output.

translation: the synthesis of proteins from mRNA by ribosomes, converting genetic code into amino acid sequences.

traveling salesman problem (TSP): the NP-complete problem of finding the shortest route visiting each location exactly once and returning to the start.

turbulence: the irregular, chaotic motion of fluids characterized by vortices and rapid changes in pressure and velocity.

Turing machine: a theoretical model of computation consisting of an infinite tape and a set of rules, capable of simulating any algorithm.

Turing test: a benchmark for artificial intelligence evaluating whether a machine's behavior is indistinguishable from that of a human.

two-player game: a strategic interaction between exactly two participants whose payoffs depend on both players' choices.

undecidable problem: a well-defined question for which no algorithm can exist that always produces a correct yes/no answer.

universal Turing machine (UTM): a Turing machine capable of simulating any other Turing machine when provided with its description and input.

unit vector: a vector of length one indicating direction only, often used to represent normalized quantities.

uncertainty principle (Heisenberg uncertainty principle): the quantum limit stating that certain pairs of observables, such as position and momentum, cannot both be known precisely.

valence electron: an outer-shell electron involved in forming chemical bonds with other atoms.

vector: a quantity that is specified by both a magnitude and a direction.

vector axis $(\vec{x}, \vec{y}, \vec{z})$: the coordinate directions defining three-dimensional space used to describe position and motion.

volcano/volcanism: the eruption of molten rock, gases, and ash through Earth's crust, forming volcanic landforms.

wave function: a mathematical object in quantum mechanics that encodes all the measurable information about a system, with its squared magnitude giving the probabilities of different outcomes.

wave-particle duality: the quantum concept that particles can exhibit both wave-like and particle-like properties depending on observation.

wobble position: the third base in a codon, where variation often does not change the encoded amino acid, providing genetic robustness.

zero-sum game: a game in which one player's gain equals the other's loss, so the total payoff across players sums to zero.

References

[1] Edward Lorenz. Predictability: Does the flap of a butterfly's wing in Brazil set off a tornado in Texas? Presented before the American Association for the Advancement of Science, December 29, 1972.

[2] NASA Goddard Space Flight Center. Solar eclipse prediction uncertainty, 2025. https://eclipse.gsfc.nasa.gov/SEcat5/uncertainty.html Accessed: 2025-02-24.

[3] Dschwen Wikimol. An icon of chaos theory – the Lorenz attractor, 2006. CC BY-SA 3.0, via Wikimedia Commons. Image modified from original.

[4] Qiang Lai, Akif Akgul, Chunbiao Li, Guanghui Xu, and Ünal Çavuşoğlu. A new chaotic system with multiple attractors: Dynamic analysis, circuit realization and s-box design. *Entropy*, 20(1), 2018. Image from figure 5(e). CC BY 4.0, modified from original.

[5] PAR. A bifurcation diagram for the logistic map, 2005. Wikimedia Commons. Public domain.

[6] Wang Sang Koon, Martin W. Lo, Jerrold E. Marsden, and Shane D. Ross. Heteroclinic connections between periodic orbits and resonance transitions in celestial mechanics. *Chaos*, 10(2):427–469, 2000.

[7] C. Fukushima and J. Westerweel. False color image of the far field of a submerged turbulent jet, 2007. CC BY 3.0, via Wikimedia Commons. Image modified from original.

[8] James Gleick. *Chaos: Making a New Science*. Viking, 1987.

[9] Ian Stewart. *Does God Play Dice?: The New Mathematics of Chaos*. Blackwell, 2nd edition, 2002.

[10] Edward K. Blum and Sergey V. Lototsky. *Mathematics of Physics and Engineering*. World Scientific Publishing Company, 2006.

[11] Albert Abraham Michelson and Edward Williams Morley. On the relative motion of the Earth and the luminiferous ether. *American Journal of Science*, 3(203):333–345, 1887.

[12] Albert Einstein. Ether and the theory of relativity. In Michel Janssen, John D. Norton, Jürgen Renn, Tilman Sauer, and John Stachel,

editors, *The Genesis of General Relativity*, pages 1537–1542. Springer, 2007.

[13] Galileo Galilei. *Dialogo di Galileo Galilei Linceo (Dialogue by Galileo Galilei Linceo)*. Batista Landini and House of Liechtenstein and Lessing J. Rosenwald Collection, Fiorenza, 1632.

[14] Joseph Carl Hafele and Richard E. Keating. Around-the-world atomic clocks: Observed relativistic time gains. *Science*, 177(4044):168–170, 1972.

[15] Bruno Rossi and David B. Hall. Variation of the rate of decay of mesotrons with momentum. *Physical Review*, 59:223–228, February 1941.

[16] Jino John 1996. A muon particle passing through lead in a cloud chamber, 2022. CC BY-SA 4.0, via Wikimedia Commons. Image modified from original.

[17] Charles Augustin Coulomb. Premier mémoire sur l'électricité et le magnétisme (First memoir on electricity and magnetism). *Histoire de l'Académie Royale des Sciences*, 569, 1785.

[18] Douglas Morrison. A drawing of a left hand illustrating Fleming's left hand rule, 2006. CC BY-SA 3.0, via Wikimedia Commons. Image modified from original.

[19] Douglas Morrison. A drawing of a right hand illustrating Fleming's right hand rule, 2006. CC BY-SA 3.0, via Wikimedia Commons. Image modified from original.

[20] Jfmelero. Illustration of the right hand rule, 2008. CC BY-SA 4.0, via Wikimedia Commons. Image modified from original.

[21] John Ambrose Fleming. *Magnets and Electric Currents*. Spon and Chamberlain, 1902.

[22] James Clerk Maxwell. *A Treatise on Electricity and Magnetism*, volume 1. Clarendon Press, 1873.

[23] André-Marie Ampère. *Mémoire sur la théorie mathématique des phénomènes électrodynamiques uniquement déduite de l'expérience (Memoir on the Mathematical Theory of Electrodynamic Phenomena, Uniquely Deduced from Experience)*. Didot, 1820.

[24] Michael Faraday. *Experimental Researches in Electricity*. R. Taylor & W. Francis, London, 1839–1855. 3 vols.; originally published in three volumes (Vol. I: 1839, Vol. II: 1844, Vol. III: 1855).

[25] Albert Einstein. Die Grundlage der allgemeinen Relativitätstheorie (The foundation of the general theory of relativity). *Annalen der Physik*, 49(7):769–822, 1916.

[26] B. Cox and J. Forshaw. *Why Does* $E=mc^2$*? (And Why Should We Care?)*. Da Capo Press, 2009.

[27] Albert Einstein. *Relativity: The Special and the General Theory.* Three Rivers Press, 1961.

[28] Edsger W. Dijkstra. *Selected Writings on Computing: A Personal Perspective.* Springer Science & Business Media, 2012.

[29] David Hilbert. Mathematische Probleme (Mathematical problems). *Nachrichten von der Gesellschaft der Wissenschaften zu Göttingen, Mathematisch-Physikalische Klasse,* 1900:253–297, 1900.

[30] David Hilbert and Wilhelm Ackermann. *Grundzüge der Theoretischen Logik (Basics of Theoretical Logic).* J. Springer, 1928.

[31] Kurt Gödel. Über formal unentscheidbare Sätze der Principia Mathematica und verwandter Systeme I (On formally undecidable theorems of principia mathematica and related systems I). *Monatshefte für Mathematik und Physik,* 38:173–198, 1931.

[32] Alan M. Turing. On computable numbers, with an application to the Entscheidungsproblem. *Journal of Mathematics,* 58(345–363):5, 1936.

[33] E. F. Moore. A simplified universal Turing machine. In *Proceedings of the 1952 ACM National Meeting (Toronto) (ACM '52),* pages 50–54. Association for Computing Machinery, 1952. https://doi.org/10.1145/800259.808993

[34] Rocky Acosta. Turing Machine, reconstructed by Mike Davey as seen at Go Ask ALICE at Harvard University, 2012. CC BY 3.0, via Wikimedia Commons. Image modified from original.

[35] Georg Cantor. Ueber eine elementare Frage der Mannigfaltigkeitslehre (On an elementary question of the theory of manifoldness). *Jahresbericht der Deutschen Mathematiker-Vereinigung,* 1:72–78, 1891.

[36] Henry Gordon Rice. Classes of recursively enumerable sets and their decision problems. *Transactions of the American Mathematical Society,* 74(2):358–366, 1953.

[37] Juris Hartmanis and Richard E. Stearns. On the computational complexity of algorithms. *Transactions of the American Mathematical Society,* 117:285–306, 1965.

[38] John Maynard Keynes. *A Tract on Monetary Reform.* Cosimo Classics, 1923.

[39] Alan Cobham. The intrinsic computational difficulty of functions. In Yehoshua Bar-Hillel, editor, *Logic, Methodology and Philosophy of Science,* pages 24–30. North-Holland Pub. Co., 1965.

[40] Jack Edmonds. Paths, trees, and flowers. *Canadian Journal of Mathematics,* 17:449–467, 1965.

[41] Michael O. Rabin. Mathematical theory of automata. In *Proceedings of the Symposium on Applied Mathematics*, volume 19, pages 153–175. American Mathematical Society, 1967.

[42] Arthur Stanley Eddington. The constants of nature. *J. R. Newman: The World of Mathematics*, 2:1074–1093, 1956.

[43] Thore Husfeldt. A TSP tour from an 1832 book, 2023. CC BY 3.0, via Wikimedia Commons.

[44] B. F. Voigt. *Der Handlungsreisende: Wie Er Sein Soll Und Was Er Zu Thun Hat, Um Aufträge Zu Erhalten Und Eines Glücklichen Erfolgs in Seinen Geschäften Gewiß Zu Sein (The Travelling Salesman: How He Should Be and What He Must Do to Obtain Orders and Be Certain of a Happy Success in His Business)*. Ilmenau, 1832.

[45] Richard M. Karp. Reducibility among combinatorial problems. In *Complexity of Computer Computations*, pages 85–103. Springer, 1972.

[46] Arkady Bolotin. Computational solution to quantum foundational problems. *arXiv preprint arXiv:1403.7686*, 2014.

[47] Whitfield Diffie and Martin E. Hellman. New directions in cryptography. *IEEE Transactions on Information Theory*, 22(6), 1976.

[48] Alan M. Turing. Computing machinery and intelligence. *Mind*, 59(236):433, 1950.

[49] Qiaozhu Mei, Yutong Xie, Walter Yuan, and Matthew O. Jackson. A Turing test of whether AI chatbots are behaviorally similar to humans. *Proceedings of the National Academy of Sciences*, 121(9):e2313925121, 2024.

[50] Patrick J. Grother and K. K. Hanaoka. NIST special database 19. *Handprinted forms and Characters Database, National Institute of Standards and Technology*, 10:69, 1995.

[51] Loc Vu-Quoc. Neuron and myelinated axon, 2018. CC BY-SA 3.0, via Wikimedia Commons. Image modified from original.

[52] Warren S. McCulloch and Walter Pitts. A logical calculus of the ideas immanent in nervous activity. *Bulletin of Mathematical Biophysics*, 5:115–133, 1943.

[53] Frank Rosenblatt. The perceptron: A probabilistic model for information storage and organization in the brain. *Psychological Review*, 65(6):386–408, 1958.

[54] Frank Rosenblatt. The design of an intelligent automaton. *Research Trends*, VI(2):1–8, 1958. Contains the original description of the perceptron and the quoted statement on p. 1.

[55] Marvin Minsky and Seymour Papert. *Perceptrons: An Introduction to Computational Geometry*. MIT Press, 1969.

[56] David E. Rumelhart, Geoffrey E. Hinton, and Ronald J. Williams. Learning representations by back-propagating errors. *Nature*, 323:533–536, 1986.

[57] Niels Bohr. *Atomic Physics and Human Knowledge*. John Wiley & Sons, Inc., 1958.

[58] Thomas Young. I. The Bakerian lecture. Experiments and calculations relative to physical optics. *Philosophical Transactions of the Royal Society of London*, 94:1–16, 1804.

[59] Jordgette. Results from the double slit experiment: Pattern from a single slit vs. a double slit, 2010. CC BY-SA 3.0, via Wikimedia Commons. Image modified from original.

[60] Arthur H. Compton. A quantum theory of the scattering of x-rays by light elements. *Physical Review*, 21(5):483, 1923.

[61] Louis de Broglie. Researches on the quantum theory. *Annalen der Physik*, 3:22–32, 1925.

[62] Yaakov Y. Fein, Philipp Geyer, Patrick Zwick, et al. Quantum superposition of molecules beyond 25 kDa. *Nature Physics*, 15(12):1242–1245, 2019.

[63] M. Jammer. *The Philosophy of Quantum Mechanics: The Interpretations of Quantum Mechanics in Historical Perspective*. Wiley, 1974.

[64] Richard Feynman. The character of physical law (1965). *Cox and Wyman Ltd.*, 1967.

[65] Richard P. Feynman, Robert B. Leighton, and Matthew Sands. *The Feynman Lectures on Physics, Volume III*. Addison-Wesley, 1963. Chapter 5: "The Schrödinger Equation in a Classical Context: A Seminar on Superconductivity".

[66] David Z. Albert. *Quantum Mechanics and Experience*. Harvard University Press, 1994.

[67] LIGO Scientific Collaboration and Virgo Collaboration. Observation of gravitational waves from a binary black hole merger. *Physical Review Letters*, 116:061102, February 2016.

[68] Ludwig Zehnder. Ein neuer Interferenzrefraktor (A new interference refractor). *Zeitschrift für Instrumentenkunde*, 11:275–285, 1891.

[69] Ludwig Mach. Ueber einen Interferenzrefraktor (On an interference refractor). *Zeitschrift für Instrumentenkunde*, 12(3):89, 1892.

[70] Walther Gerlach and Otto Stern. Der experimentelle Nachweis der Richtungsquantelung im Magnetfeld (The experimental proof of directional quantization in the magnetic field). *Zeitschrift für Physik*, 9(1):349–352, December 1922.

[71] Werner Heisenberg. Über den anschaulichen Inhalt der quantentheoretischen Kinematik und Mechanik (On the illustrative content

of quantum theoretical kinematics and mechanics). *Zeitschrift für Physik*, 43(3):172–198, 1927.

[72] David Deutsch. Quantum theory, the Church–Turing principle and the universal quantum computer. *Proceedings of the Royal Society of London. A. Mathematical and Physical Sciences*, 400(1818):97–117, 1985.

[73] Gregor Mendel. Versuche über Pflanzen-hybriden (Experiments in plant hybridization). *Verhandlungen des Naturforschenden Vereines in Brünn*, 4:3–47, 1866.

[74] Lewis Thomas. *A Long Line of Cells: Collected Essays*. Book-of-the-Month Club, 1990.

[75] Edmund B. Wilson. *The Cell in Development and Heredity*. Macmillan, 3rd edition, 1925.

[76] Thomas Hunt Morgan. Sex limited inheritance in Drosophila. *Science*, 32(812):120–122, July 1910.

[77] Richard Wheeler. The major chromatin structures, 2005. CC BY-SA 3.0, via Wikimedia Commons. Image modified from original.

[78] Pierre Maguin and Luciano A. Marraffini. From the discovery of DNA to current tools for DNA editing. *Journal of Experimental Medicine*, 218(4), 2021.

[79] Oswald T. Avery, Colin M. MacLeod, and Maclyn McCarty. Studies on the chemical nature of the substance inducing transformation of pneumococcal types: Induction of transformation by a desoxyribonucleic acid fraction isolated from pneumococcus type III. *Journal of Experimental Medicine*, 79(2):137–158, 1944.

[80] A. D. Hershey and Martha Chase. Independent functions of viral protein and nucleic acid in growth of bacteriophage. *Journal of General Physiology*, 36(1):39–56, September 1952.

[81] Cold Spring Harbor Laboratory DNA Learning Center. Gallery 19: DNA model, 1953. Courtesy of the BGI Nobel Laureates Archives, Cold Spring Harbor Laboratory, New York.

[82] National Human Genome Research Institute. The structure of DNA, 2006. Public domain.

[83] J. D. Watson and F. H. C. Crick. Molecular structure of nucleic acids: A structure for deoxyribose nucleic acid. *Nature*, 171:737–738, April 1953.

[84] F. H. C. Crick. On protein synthesis. In F. K. Sanders, editor, *Symposia of the Society for Experimental Biology, Number XII: The Biological Replication of Macromolecules*, pages 138–163. Cambridge University Press, 1958.

[85] National Human Genome Research Institute. Reworked and vectorized by Sulai. DNA transcription, 2009. Wikimedia Commons. Public Domain. Image modified from original.

[86] François Jacob and Jacques Monod. Genetic regulatory mechanisms in the synthesis of proteins. *Journal of Molecular Biology*, 3:318–356, 1961.

[87] International Human Genome Sequencing Consortium. Finishing the euchromatic sequence of the human genome. *Nature*, 431:931–945, 2004.

[88] Samuel Butler. *Erewhon; Or, Over the Range*. Trübner & Co., 1872. Chapter 24: "The Book of the Machines".

[89] John von Neumann and Arthur W. Burks (Ed.). *Theory of Self-Reproducing Automata*. University of Illinois Press, 1966.

[90] National Human Genome Research Institute. The four classes of protein structure, 2010. Public Domain. Image modified from original.

[91] Christian B. Anfinsen. Principles that govern the folding of protein chains. *Science*, 181(4096):223–230, 1973.

[92] John Jumper, Richard Evans, Alexander Pritzel, et al. Highly accurate protein structure prediction with AlphaFold. *Nature*, 596(7873):583–589, August 2021.

[93] Ewen Callaway. 'It will change everything': DeepMind's AI makes gigantic leap in solving protein structures. *Nature*, 588(7837):203–204, December 2020.

[94] Yoshizumi Ishino, Hideo Shinagawa, Kozo Makino, Mitsuko Amemura, and Atsuo Nakata. Nucleotide sequence of the iap gene, responsible for alkaline phosphatase isozyme conversion in Escherichia coli, and identification of the gene product. *Journal of Bacteriology*, 169(12):5429–5433, 1987.

[95] Martin Jinek, Krzysztof Chylinski, Ines Fonfara, et al. A programmable dual-RNA-guided DNA endonuclease in adaptive bacterial immunity. *Science*, 337(6096):816–821, 2012.

[96] Le Cong, F. Ann Ran, David Cox, et al. Multiplex genome engineering using CRISPR/Cas systems. *Science*, 339(6121):819–823, 2013.

[97] Prashant Mali, Luhan Yang, Kevin M. Esvelt, et al. RNA-guided human genome engineering via Cas9. *Science*, 339(6121):823–826, 2013.

[98] George Gamow. Possible relation between deoxyribonucleic acid and protein structures. *Nature*, 173:318, 1954.

[99] Theodosius Dobzhansky. Nothing in biology makes sense except in the light of evolution. *The American Biology Teacher*, 35(3):125–129, March 1973.

[100] Nina M. Davies (copyist). Queen Nefertari playing Senet, Circa 1279–1213. Wikimedia Commons. Public Domain. Image modified from original.

[101] Remke Kruk. Of rukhs and rooks, camels and castles. *Oriens*, 36(1):288–298, 2001.

[102] J. von Neumann. Zur Theorie der Gesellschaftsspiele (On the theory of games of strategy). *Mathematische Annalen*, 100(1):295–320, 1928.

[103] Thomas Dohmen and Hendrik Sonnabend. Further field evidence for minimax play. *Journal of Sports Economics*, 19(3):371–388, 2018.

[104] John F. Nash. Equilibrium points in n-person games. *Proceedings of the National Academy of Sciences*, 36(1):48–49, 1950.

[105] R. Duncan Luce and Howard Raiffa. *Games and Decisions: An Introduction and Critical Survey*. Wiley & Sons, 1957. Chapter 5, Section 3.

[106] Steven Kuhn. Prisoner's dilemma. *The Stanford Encyclopedia of Philosophy*, 2019. Accessed: 2025-03-16.

[107] W. Poundstone. *Prisoner's Dilemma: John von Neumann, Game Theory, and the Puzzle of the Bomb*. Doubleday, 1992.

[108] Robert J. Aumann. Acceptable points in general cooperative n-person games. *Contributions to the Theory of Games*, 4(40):287–324, 1959.

[109] Robert Axelrod. Effective choice in the prisoner's dilemma. *Journal of Conflict Resolution*, 24(1):3–25, 1980.

[110] Shirli Kopelman. Tit for tat and beyond: The legendary work of Anatol Rapoport. *Negotiation and Conflict Management Research*, 13(1):60–84, 2020.

[111] Robert Axelrod. More effective choice in the prisoner's dilemma. *Journal of Conflict Resolution*, 24(3):379–403, 1980.

[112] Drew Fudenberg and Eric Maskin. The folk theorem in repeated games with discounting or with incomplete information. *Econometrica*, 54(3):533–554, 1986.

[113] Gilbert Roberts. Cooperation: How vampire bats build reciprocal relationships. *Current Biology*, 30(7):R307–R309, 2020.

[114] Tatjana Krama, Jolanta Vrublevska, Todd M. Freeberg, et al. You mob my owl, I'll mob yours: Birds play tit-for-tat game. *Scientific Reports*, 2(1):800, 2012.

[115] J. Maynard Smith and George R. Price. The logic of animal conflict. *Nature*, 246(5427):15–18, 1973.

[116] Robert Axelrod and William D. Hamilton. The evolution of cooperation. *Science*, 211(4489):1390–1396, 1981.

[117] Paul Milgrom. *Putting Auction Theory to Work*. Cambridge University Press, 2004.

[118] Tim Roughgarden and Éva Tardos. How bad is selfish routing? *Journal of the ACM*, 49(2):236–259, 2002.

[119] William S. Vickrey. Congestion theory and transport investment. *American Economic Review*, 59(2):251–260, 1969.

[120] Noam Brown and Tuomas Sandholm. Superhuman AI for multiplayer poker. *Science*, 365(6456):885–890, 2019.

[121] M. Ridley. *The Red Queen: Sex and the Evolution of Human Nature*. Penguin Books, 1995.

[122] James Jeans. The mysterious universe. *The British Journal of Radiology*, 4(43):351–354, 1931.

[123] Carl Sagan. *The Cosmic Connection: An Extraterrestrial Perspective*. Doubleday, 1973.

[124] Steffen Reinbothe, Christiane Reinbothe, Klaus Apel, and Nikolai Lebedev. Evolution of chlorophyll biosynthesis – the challenge to survive photooxidation. *Cell*, 86(5):703–705, 1996.

[125] At09kg. The overall process of photosynthesis, 2011. CC BY-SA 3.0, via Wikimedia Commons. Image in the book is inspired from the original.

[126] Evans Love. This is a diagram depicting a large set of human metabolic pathways, 2016. CC BY-SA 4.0, via Wikimedia Commons. Image modified from original.

[127] Craig M. Schiffries, Andrea Johnson Mangum, Jennifer L. Mays, et al. The Deep Carbon Observatory: A ten-year quest to study carbon in Earth. *Engineering*, 5(3):372–378, 2019.

[128] Michael Ghil and Denisse Sciamarella. Dynamical systems, algebraic topology and the climate sciences. *Nonlinear Processes in Geophysics*, 30(4):399–434, 2023.

[129] W. F. Libby. Atmospheric helium three and radiocarbon from cosmic radiation. *Physical Review*, 69:671–672, June 1946.

[130] James R. Arnold and Willard F. Libby. Age determinations by radiocarbon content: checks with samples of known age. *Science*, 110(2869):678–680, 1949.

[131] J. Barnett and R. Hoffman. *Carbon: One Atom's Odyssey*. No Starch Press, 2021.

[132] Primo Levi. *The Periodic Table*. Schocken Books, 1984.

[133] David Beerling. *The Emerald Planet: How Plants Changed Earth's History*. Oxford Landmark Science. Oxford University Press, 2017.

[134] William Thomson. The age of the Earth. *Nature*, 51:438–440, 1895.

[135] National Aeronautics and Space Administration. The internal structure of terrestrial planets, 2003. NASA. Public Domain. Image modified from original.

[136] U.S. Geological Survey. Snider-Pellegrini Wegener fossil map, 1999. USGS. Public Domain. Image modified from original.

[137] Alfred Wegener. Die Entstehung der Kontinente (The formation of the continents). *Geologische Rundschau*, 3(4):276–292, 1912.

[138] Harry H. Hess. History of ocean basins. In A. E. J. Engel, Harold L. James, and B. F. Leonard, editors, *Petrologic Studies: A Volume in Honor of A. F. Buddington*, pages 599–620. Geological Society of America, 1962. Special Paper.

[139] F. J. Vine and D. H. Matthews. Magnetic anomalies over oceanic ridges. *Nature*, 199:947–949, 1963.

[140] M. Bitton. Map of Earth's principal tectonic plates. 2013. CC BY-SA 3.0, via Wikimedia Commons. Image modified from original.

[141] National Parks Gallery. Earthquake and volcanic activity, 2019. NPS. Public Domain. Image modified from original.

[142] Mapbliss. Map of the main islands of Hawaii, 2015. CC BY-SA 4.0, via Wikimedia Commons. Image modified from original.

[143] National Park Service. Map of Columbia Plateau and Snake River Plain volcanic features, 2022. NPS. Public Domain. Image modified from original.

[144] Abraham Ortelius. *Thesaurus Geographicus, Recognitus et Auctus (Geographical Thesaurus, Revised and Enlarged)*. Ex officina Christophori Plantini, Antverpiae, 1596. Expanded 2nd edition.

[145] Mario Livio. *Brilliant Blunders: From Darwin to Einstein – Colossal Mistakes by Great Scientists That Changed Our Understanding of Life and the Universe*. Simon & Schuster, 2013.

[146] Nigel Calder. *The Restless Earth: A Report on the New Geology*. Viking Press, 1972.

[147] John McPhee. *Annals of the Former World*. Farrar, Straus and Giroux, 1998. Winner of the 1999 Pulitzer Prize for General Nonfiction.

For EU product safety concerns, contact us at Calle de José Abascal, 56–1°, 28003 Madrid, Spain or eugpsr@cambridge.org.

www.ingramcontent.com/pod-product-compliance
Lightning Source LLC
LaVergne TN
LVHW010722061126
851857LV00014B/1303
9781009711197